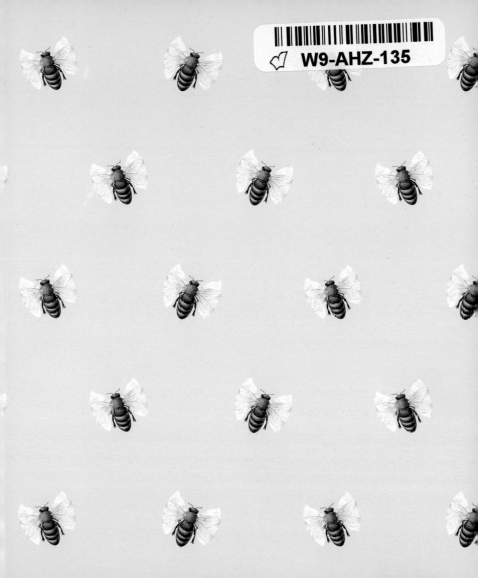

NEW JERSEY

ART OF THE STATE

ART OF THE STATE

NEW JERSEY

The Spirit of America

Text by Robert Heide and John Gilman

Harry N. Abrams, Inc., Publishers

NEW YORK

This book was prepared for publication at
Walking Stick Press, San Francisco

Project staff:
Series Designer: Linda Herman
Series Editor: Diana Landau
Consulting Writer: Nancy Friedman

For Harry N. Abrams, Inc.:
Series Editor: Ruth A. Peltason

Page 1: *Cityscape* (collage view of Trenton) by Hughie Lee-Smith, 1988.
New Jersey State Council on the Arts. Photo Dan Dragan

Page 2: *Dancing on the George Washington Bridge* by Faith Ringgold, 1988.
Private collection

Library of Congress Cataloguing-in-Publication Data
Gilman, John, 1941–.
New Jersey / text by John Gilman and Robert Heide.
p.   cm. — (Art of the state)
ISBN 0–8109–5566–0
1. New Jersey Miscellanea.   2. New Jersey Pictorial works.
I. Heide, Robert, 1939–   II. Title.   II. Series.
F134.G55   1999
974.9—dc21   99–28807

Harry N. Abrams, Inc.   Abrams is a subsidiary of
100 Fifth Avenue
New York, N.Y. 10011   LA MARTINIÈRE
www.abramsbooks.com   G R O U P E

Autumn, New Jersey by John Marin, 1913. *Richard York Gallery, New York*

"Say what you will…New Jersey is resilient….

The same self-confidence which some people wrongly call conceit carries Jerseymen from despondency to merriment. All that is needed is a touch of friendly sun, a good crop in the garden, and an off-sea breeze."

Harry Emerson Wildes, Twin Rivers: The Raritan and the Passaic, *1943*

Wedged between the powerful port cities of New York and Philadelphia, New Jersey has always known the middle child's struggle to be noticed and loved on its own merits. New Jersey was, in Ben Franklin's memorable phrase, "a keg tapped at both ends," but it was no empty vessel. Its strategic position made it a fiercely contested battleground during the Revolutionary War. Its "in-between" status gave rise to great transportation systems, and its enterprise led to marvelous industrial innovations. On the other hand, New Jersey—too often the punch line of bad jokes—has never taken itself all that seriously. Jerseyans savor their offbeat pleasures, from roadside diners to the Miss America pageant to the 250-year-old legend of the Jersey Devil, an imp held responsible for every mishap in the state.

Jerseyans also are justifiably proud of their state's diversity, which starts with its geography. Although it's the only state in which every county is considered "metropolitan" by the U.S. Census, New Jersey still has wilderness in the Kittatinny Mountains of the northwest and the mysterious, sparsely settled Pine Barrens of the south—the single largest wilderness area on the East Coast. New Jersey still has enough farming to back up its old nickname, "The Garden State," and enough resorts along the 127-mile Atlantic shore to delight vacationers of every stripe, from high-rolling

Space Motive, a N. J. Valley by Oscar Bluemner, c. 1917–18. *Whitney Museum of American Art, New York*

gamblers to families seeking affordable leisure on the beaches and boardwalks.

From its beginnings as a colony, New Jersey could boast of its diverse population. Dutch traders and trappers settled here first, in the early 17th century, followed soon by Swedish Lutherans and British Puritans and Quakers. German, Italian, and Irish immigrants filled New Jersey's cities in the mid-19th century, freed slaves flooded in after the Civil War, and Jews from Eastern Europe arrived toward the end of the century. In the 1950s and 1960s, an influx of Cubans and Puerto Ricans joined a vibrant ethnic mix that today includes Russians, Scots, Poles, Swiss, and newcomers from many other lands. New Jersey's high-tech and pharmaceutical industries attract upwardly mobile Americans from other states, as well as skilled workers from Asia and the former Soviet bloc.

Places whose inhabitants come mostly from "outside" often share a restless, striving energy that promotes creativity and industry. In this way, New Jersey may be more like California or Washington State and less like its northeastern neighbors. An astonishing number of musicians and poets—from Count Basie to Frank Sinatra to Bruce Springsteen, from William Carlos Williams to Allen Ginsberg to Robert Pinsky—were born here, suggesting a lyrical essence in the Jersey air. Reversing the historic "go west" trend, Thomas Edison came here from Ohio and created the electric light, the motion-picture camera, and many other groundbreaking inventions. Bell Labs in Murray Hill, Union, and Holmdel has been a telecommunications pioneer for decades; Princeton University's Institute for Advanced Studies has nurtured the world's brilliant thinkers, including Albert Einstein and Robert Oppenheimer. The Singer Sewing Machine Company, Johnson & Johnson, and the Campbell Soup Company—all innovators in their fields—grew from New Jersey soil; and the landmarks of Jersey's industrial corridor inspired painter John Marin and others.

Commerce has been a blight as well as a blessing to New Jersey. Concrete, factories, and effluent don't make for scenic vistas, and for a time the state became synonymous with rampant industrialization. That view is changing now, as New Jersey moves to protect its great natural resources. Thanks to federal mandates, many waste areas have been reclaimed and transformed. The ocean and beaches have never been cleaner; open lands are being set aside for the state's environmental heritage. And the town of Hoboken, Sinatra's birthplace, was

Miss America in a convertible. *Photo Walter Choroszewski*

itself reborn in the last few decades. Its 19th-century buildings are being restored, and its one-mile-square environs vie for appeal with New York's Greenwich Village.

In the arts, too, New Jersey is experiencing a rebirth. Whereas writers once chose anything *but* their home state for subject matter, today novelists such as Tom De Haven (*Jersey Luck*), Richard Ford (*The Sportswriter*), and James Kaplan (*Two Guys from Verona*), as well as filmmakers such as Todd Solondz and Kevin Smith, are setting their works in the familiar milieus of suburb, turnpike, and shore. Studios and galleries in former industrial sites show important work by local artists, museums have revitalized their collections, and the state arts council sponsors lively projects for public spaces. No longer beleaguered by inferiority, New Jerseyans take pride in their state's rich past and exciting present—and satisfaction in finding everything they could want right in their own backyard. ❧

NEW JERSEY

"The Garden State"
3rd State

Date of Statehood
DECEMBER 18, 1787

Capital
TRENTON

Bird
EASTERN GOLDFINCH

Flower
COMMON MEADOW VIOLET

Tree
RED OAK

Insect
HONEYBEE

Animal
HORSE

Fish
BROOK TROUT

There are two New Jerseys, represented by two sets of symbols. The official New Jersey is a state of proud heritage and quiet industry. Its flag is descended from a 1780 standard whose buff and dark blue colors, chosen by George Washington during the Revolution, came from the insignia of the Netherlands (the Dutch were early settlers here). On the seal, a plow, a horse, and Ceres—Greek goddess of agriculture—symbolize the land's bounty. The meadow violet is modest and maidenly; the red oak sturdy and enduring; the knobbed whelk ubiquitous on the state's beaches and bays.

Eastern goldfinch and common meadow violet

The unofficial symbols tell a contrasting story: offbeat, eccentric, and about as dignified as Atlantic City on a summer weekend. New Jersey even has a state dinosaur, *Hadrosaurus*

State seal

"Liberty and Prosperity"

State motto

foulkii, because the first fossil of this animal was found in Haddonfield in 1858. Not just the sedate "Garden State," New Jersey is also known less flatteringly as the Commuter State, the Turnpike State, and the Factory State. And its semiofficial landmarks, from the Edison Tower to Lucy the Margate Elephant, have a surreal quality that's closer to Hollywood than to the Liberty Bell. ❧

The Jersey Devil

New Jersey is the only state that can claim an official demon, not to be confused with its official animal. The Jersey Devil is said to have been born in 1735 to a Mrs. Leeds,

THE JERSEY DEVIL

who, having already borne 12 children, wished aloud that her next-born would be a devil. Sure enough, after its birth the creature flew up the chimney and out into the Pine Barrens, where its screams and moans are heard to this day. The Jersey Devil is reported to be cloven-hoofed, long-tailed, and reddish-brown, with the head of a crested hawk, a horselike face, the body of a kangaroo, and the wings of a bat.

Above: Litho print of the Edison Tower in Menlo Park, a New Jersey landmark. *Left:* Vintage depiction of the Jersey Devil. The legend lives on in the name of the New Jersey Devils, a National Hockey League team based in the Meadowlands Sports Complex. *Both, Robert Heide and John Gilman*

Tuneless in Trenton

Alone of all the 50 states, New Jersey has no official state song, despite legislative attempts to name one in 1940, 1954, and 1970. Even a 1980 effort to designate native son Bruce Springsteen's "Born to Run" (which, ironically, celebrates leaving New Jersey) as the state's unofficial rock 'n' roll song failed for lack of legislative action. Not that New Jersey lacks for musical tributes. At least six songs have been written about the New Jersey Turnpike alone, and tunes from World War II's "Jersey Bounce" to "Ho-ho-Hoboken" to Sinatra's 1980 tribute "Before the Music Ends" have saluted New Jersey cheerfully, wittily, and movingly.

Above: "I Love the State of New Jersey" sheet music cover, c. 1921. *Robert Heide and John Gilman. Right:* The New Jersey State House, polychromatic postcard, c. 1935. The state capitol at Trenton was built in the French Renaissance style around 1792, and enlarged and altered many times. The gilded dome was added in 1889 after a fire. *State House Collection*

"I Like Jersey Best"

The Pinelands and the Vinelands
Seaside Heights, Margate
You can have Miami
I love the Garden State
I've been a lot of places
seen pictures of the rest
but of all the places I can think of
I like Jersey best.

Chorus from "I Like Jersey Best," words and music by J. Cosgriff,
recorded by John Pizzarelli, Jr. Cosgriff's
"hymn to that much-maligned state"
was proposed in 1983 as the official
state jingle (not song) but has yet to
win official recognition.

Above: New Jersey has an official
shell, the knobbed whelk. *Photo M. H.
Sharp/Photo Researchers, Inc.* **Left:** Red
oak leaves. *Photo Walter Choroszewski.*
Right: Campbell Kid from 1926 promotional booklet. The "Kids" were created in 1904 by artist Grace Gebble
Drayton. *Robert Heide and John Gilman*

Soupe "Le Bijou" à la Campbell's

1 can Campbell's condensed
   Tomato Soup
1 can Campbell's condensed
   Cream of Mushroom Soup
1 soupcan whole milk
1 soupcan light cream
2 tbsp. dry sherry
½ tsp. melted butter
Dash of white pepper
Chopped parsley for garnish

Empty canned soups into sauce-
pan. Add milk and light cream
and mix together over a low
flame, stirring often to avoid
scalding. Add sherry, butter,
and white pepper; heat just to
the boiling point. Pour into
soup bowls and garnish with
chopped parsley. Serves four.

c. 10,000 B.C. First Native American people settle in what is now New Jersey.

1524 Giovanni da Verrazano explores the New Jersey shore around Newark Bay.

1609 Henry Hudson explores the New Jersey Shore and the Hudson River, claiming the region for the Netherlands.

1618 Dutch traders establish first European settlement in New Jersey, at Bergen.

1642 America's first brewery established in Hoboken.

1664 King Charles II of England grants Dutch lands in America to his brother James. A British fleet takes possession of the territory without firing a shot; the area west of the Hudson becomes known as New Jersey.

1676 New Jersey is divided into East Jersey, which belongs to a royal supporter, Sir George Carteret; and West Jersey, bought by Quakers led by William Penn.

1702 East and West Jersey united as a British crown colony but governed from New York.

1746 College of New Jersey (Princeton University) is chartered.

1758 Brotherton, the first Indian reservation in North America, founded at Indian Mills for New Jersey's surviving Lenape people.

1766 Queens College (Rutgers University) is founded.

1776 General George Washington and his troops cross the Delaware and defeat King George III's Hessian mercenaries at Trenton.

1777–1780 Significant conflicts with the British at Princeton, Monmouth, and Springfield.

1787 New Jersey becomes third state to ratify the U.S. Constitution.

1790 Population 184,139.

1791 Paterson founded as first planned industrial city in the U.S.

1804 An act for the gradual abolition of slavery in New Jersey is passed.

1811 World's first ferry service begins between Hoboken and Manhattan.

1825 First railroad in America is operated in Hoboken, on a circular track.

1830 Population 320,823.

1834 Delaware–Raritan Canal is completed from Philadelphia to New York City.

1840 First radio signal is transmitted at Princeton.

1846 World's first baseball game is played in Hoboken.

1860 Population 672,035.

FIFTY ONE YEARS of QUALITY

1862 Fort Delaware becomes a prison for captured Confederates; New Jersey will send 88,306 men to the Union Army.

1870 World's first boardwalk is built in Atlantic City.

1877 Thomas Edison makes first phonograph recording at his Menlo Park laboratory.

1880 Population 1,131,116.

1897 World's first "condensed" soup created in Camden County.

1907–1917 Fort Lee is capital of motion-picture industry.

1910 Population 2,537,167.

1921 First Miss America pageant held in Atlantic City.

1926–27 Delaware River Bridge and Holland Tunnel open, linking New Jersey, Philadelphia, and New York.

1930 Population 4,041,334.

1931 George Washington Bridge opens between Fort Lee and Manhattan.

1932 Infant son of aviator Charles Lindbergh is kidnapped and later found dead near Hopewell.

1933 First national historical park opens at Morristown; nation's first drive-in movie theater opens in Camden County.

1937 German dirigible *Hindenburg* explodes while trying to land at Lakehurst.

1941–1945 Fort Dix handles 1.3 million draftees for WWII.

1950 Population 4,835,329.

1951 New Jersey Turnpike opens from the George Washington Bridge to Camden.

1955 Garden State Parkway is completed from Montville to Cape May.

1960 Population 6,067,412.

1976 Meadowlands Sports Complex opens in East Rutherford.

1978 Casino gambling begins in Atlantic City.

1984 State files federal suit contending that it owns Ellis and Liberty Islands. (The suit is eventually decided in New Jersey's favor.)

1987 New Jerseyan Richard Purdy Wilbur named U.S. poet laureate.

1990 Population 7,730,188.

1993 Christine Todd Whitman becomes first woman elected governor.

1995 New Jersey Devils capture the NHL's coveted Stanley Cup for the first time in the franchise's history.

> *"Here there is diversity, here there is contrast."*
>
> John T. Cunningham, This Is New Jersey, 1953

The Palisades by John Hill, 1823–24. Formed nearly 200 million years ago by the slow cooling of molten rock, the sheer cliffs rise as high as 550 feet above the Hudson River. *Metropolitan Museum of Art, New York*

New Jersey is America's fifth-smallest state—only Delaware, Connecticut, Hawaii, and Rhode Island are smaller—yet its 8,000 or so square miles are dramatically varied. A natural peninsula, it is bordered by the Atlantic Ocean and the Hudson River on the east and the Delaware River on the west. Sheer cliffs, lush forests, rich farmlands, highland lakes, swampy marshes, and a cove-notched coast offer startling contrast to the state's narrow urban and industrial corridors.

Much of New Jersey's variety was carved out by the Wisconsin Glacier, which inched southward 150,000 years ago and finished its retreat from present-day New Jersey about 10,000 to 20,000 years ago. The glacier shaped deep river gorges, the hills of northern New Jersey, the glacial lakes of Morris and Sussex counties, the spectacular Palisades overlooking the Hudson River, and the wetlands that form nearly 13 percent of New Jersey's land area. But after invading the state's northern third, the ice halted; southward lies a low, rolling coastal plain, part of the great eastern seaboard that extends from New York to Florida. ❧

"I HAVE TRIED, AND STILL AM TRYING, TO MAKE the people who live in New Jersey aware of all New Jersey, to persuade those whose lives have held them in the Delaware Valley to become more conscious of the sea, to make those barely aware of the flatlands to the South become more sensible of the mountains to the North, and to infuse in the boy complacent among the salt sedges of Atlantic and Cape May a longing to see…the rocky ledges of Sussex or the misty hills of Somerset."

Henry Charlton Beck, in his foreword to A New Jersey Reader, *1961*

Barnegat Lighthouse. Rebuilt in 1857–58 after the original fell into the water, the "Grand Old Champion of the Tides" surveys Barnegat Shoals off Long Beach Island, the site of more than 200 shipwrecks. *Photo Walter Choroszewski*

New Jersey's northern regions, slightly less than two-fifths of the state's area, are the foothills of the Appalachian Range. Here, in the oldest and highest part of the state, is the rugged Walpack Ridge, a wall of rock bordering the Delaware River, and the heavily forested Kittatinny Mountains, which rise to 1,804 feet at High Point—not surprisingly, the state's highest elevation. The Delaware River descends from High Point to form the natural boundary between New Jersey and Pennsylvania. From whitewater rapids at Lambertville to tidal waters from the Delaware Bay at Trenton, the river passes graceful fields and quiet marshes before it drifts lazily into the sea at Cape May, the state's southernmost tip.

South and east of the fertile Kittatinny Valley are New Jersey's

highlands. Broad, rounded, and flat-topped ridges are bisected by swift, clear rivers and streams such as the Wanaque, the Rockaway, the Pequennock, and the north and south branches of the Raritan—the largest river wholly within the state's borders. ❧

The Delaware Water Gap

One of America's great natural spectacles, the Delaware Water Gap is a deep channel cut in Precambrian times by the Delaware River as it passed through the quartzite rock of the Kittatinny

Mountains. Flanked by 1,200-foot peaks and nearly a mile wide at its extremes, the Gap has inspired artists from George Inness onward. Its rugged grandeur is softened by forests of oak, hickory, maple, and white pine, and in summer by lush rhododendrons and mountain laurel Since 1965 the Gap has been protected as part of the Delaware Water Gap National Recreation Area, a 70,000-acre park that runs for 37 miles along both sides of the river.

Above: The Delaware Water Gap by George Inness, 1859. The Montclair Art Museum. Opposite: **Waterfall at Delaware Water Gap.** *Photo Kelly/Mooney.* **The subject of countless paintings and photographs, the Water Gap encompasses a 25-mile portion of the Appalachian Trail.**

Maurice River and Farm-lands by David Ahlsted, 1995. The Maurice (MOR-ris) flows through the southern part of the state, near Millville and Vineland, once envisioned as the hub of a wine-growing region. *Courtesy the artist*

Farmlands and Pine Barrens

New Jersey has been known as "The Garden State" since colonial days, and though farming is less important now than in earlier decades, it is still vital to the state's economy. From the dairy farms of Burlington, Hunterdon, and Somerset counties to the field crops grown statewide, farming is small in scale yet highly productive. New Jersey is one of the nation's leading producers of tomatoes, blueberries, cranberries, spinach, and peaches.

Once considered useless wilderness, the state's swamps, bogs, and marshes today are recognized as key parts of a complex drainage system indispensable to the health of the environment. Most fascinating is the unique region known as the Pine Barrens, or Pinelands, which covers more than 1 million acres from Cape May to the southern edge of Monmouth County. Under this land lies the East Coast's largest natural aquifer, equivalent to a lake 75 feet deep and the source of some of the purest water on earth. Cranberries and blueberries flourish here, cultivated by the descendants of 17th- and 18th-century settlers.

"EVEN ON BRIGHT DAYS, THE RIVERS CAN BE DARK AND ALMOST sunless under stands of white cedar, and then, all in a moment, they run into brilliant sunshine where the banks rise higher and the forest of oak and pine is less dense."

John McPhee, The Pine Barrens, 1968

Above: Gentians in the Pine Barrens. *Photo Walter Choroszewski. Below:* Pine Barrens cranberry bog. *Photo Michael Melford.* The marshy land of the Pine Barrens is well suited to "bog berries." Local berry farmers include the descendants of Colonial army deserters, religious refugees, and other nonconformists, whose way of life has changed only slowly over the decades, as roads and schools have been introduced to the region.

Long Branch, New Jersey by Winslow Homer, 1869. Long Branch became a fashionable shore resort in the mid-19th century. In 1852, a *New York Herald* writer observed, "Those who like a spice of everything should patronize Long Branch." *Museum of Fine Arts, Boston*

Rarely rising more than 100 feet above sea level, New Jersey's Coastal Plain extends 127 miles, from the Atlantic Highlands and the 6½-mile barrier beach of Sandy Hook to the Cape May peninsula. Known to New Jerseyans simply as "the Shore," it is an almost unbroken succession of beaches and sandbars caused by constant wave action and filigreed by rivers, inlets, bays, sounds, tidal marshes, and vast estuaries. The waves create, then inundate, a narrow chain of offshore islands. As a result, the coast is too irregular for shipping but ideal for recreation. Famous resorts such as Atlantic City, Long Branch, Asbury Park, and many others have long been magnets for residents and tourists seeking relief from the sweltering cities. ❧

"NOTHING IN NATURE IS MORE DECEPTIVE THAN THE Jersey coast. On balmy summer days, the smooth Atlantic breathes a welcome. The soft swell whispers to the sailor, luring him farther from the strand; the shimmering expanse of water…promises peace and relaxation. Beneath that silken sociability lies peril. Long, slender sandspits lurk hidden underwater… Sudden storms lash the sea into giant combers.…"

Harry Emerson Wildes, Twin Rivers: The Raritan and the Passaic, *1943*

Shark Summer

In the summer of 1916, long before *Jaws* showed its teeth, a killer shark struck terror among vacationers on the Jersey shore. The first attacks, at Beach Haven on the southern tip of Long Beach Island, resulted in several injuries and one fatality. The shark then made its way up the coast and killed its next victim at Spring Lake. Eluding capture, the creature amazingly swam through the Manasquan inlet 11 miles upstream to a freshwater pond, where it attacked and killed two young boys. A massive hunt along the eastern seaboard resulted in the capture of a huge killer shark containing human remains. On the Jersey Shore, folks still refer to that terrible season as "Shark Summer."

The Edwin B. Forsythe National Wildlife Refuge. Near Oceanville on the Atlantic coast, the refuge covers 24,000 acres of bays, channels, and tidal marshes. More than 275 species of waterfowl and other birds have been sighted there. *Photo Scott Barrow*

> *"They tread strong and clever and mostly walk with a lofty chin."*
>
> William Penn c. 1680

Henry Hudson landing on the New Jersey shore of the Hudson River, **engraving after a painting by R. W. Weir, c. 1857.** *New Jersey Historical Society. Opposite below:* **Tishcohan, chief of the Lenape people.** *Library of Congress*

The Land Along the Water

Some 10,000 years ago, nomadic Indians reached the region now called New Jersey, following the streams and rivers to a shore that lay 100 miles east of its current location. They fished the teeming sea and hunted moose, elk, caribou, musk oxen, and mammoths. Centuries later, the trails they had blazed were adopted by new, more settled groups. Although they spoke two distinct languages, they are now known by a single

Artifacts from Waterloo Village, a Lenape site. *Photo Scott Barrow*

name, Lenape, "Original People." Members of the Algonquian group, they probably had emigrated from southern Canada; by A.D. 900 they were living in small farming communities whose main crops included squash, beans, sunflowers, pumpkins, and tobacco. Fishing and hunting rounded out their diet.

Numbering no more than 10,000 at the time of European contact, the Lenape maintained largely peaceful relations with the Dutch and English. Disease and migration further reduced their numbers, and by 1758, when the New Jersey Colony purchased 3,000 acres of land in Burlington County for a reservation, only about 200 Lenape moved onto it. Brotherton, the first reservation in North America, dissolved in 1801 when its residents joined their brethren in New York State.

At first, in that place, at all times, above the earth,
On the earth, was an extended fog,
And there the great Manito was....
He made the extended land in the sky.
He made the sun, the moon, the stars.
He made them all to move evenly.
Then the wind blew violently, and it cleared,
And the water flowed off far and strong.
And groups of islands grew newly, and
    there remained.

*From the Walum Olum ("painted records"), a Lenape
picture epic engraved on bark. The artifact was discovered
and translated by Constantine Rafinesque in the early 1830s.*

Competing Claims

The first European to glimpse the Jersey shore was Giovanni da Verrazano, in 1524. Almost a century later, English navigator Henry Hudson, sailing for the Dutch East India Company, explored both sides of the river that now bears his name, and established the colony of "New Netherland." Scores of Dutch adventurers, lured by Hudson's accounts of abundant fox and otter in the Jersey woods, launched trading expeditions and in 1618 established the first European settlement in New Jersey, at Bergen.

Queen Christina of Sweden attempted to join in the bonanza, sending colonists to the Delaware River Valley in 1638. Although New Sweden failed to prosper, a few axe-wielding Finns in the group built excellent log cabins, later copied by colonists all over the continent. The most ambitious claimant was Great Britain, which in 1664, without firing a shot, took over from the Netherlands both Manhattan and the smaller colony across the river. James, Duke of York, named New Jersey for the island that had sheltered him during England's civil war and awarded it to two friends. Lord John Berkeley and Sir George Carteret divided the colony between them; ten years later, a group of Quakers led by William Penn bought Berkeley's section, "West" Jersey.

> "MY HOUSE WAS BESET, MY DOOR BROKEN DOWN,
> and my person seized in the night time by armed
> men sent to execute a paper order from the Gover-
> nor of New York, to whom I was sent a prisoner...."
>
> *John Fenwick, a Quaker who claimed ownership of one-tenth of Berkeley's West Jersey, complaining of his treatment by British authorities, c. 1676*

Philip Carteret appointed Governor of the Colony of New Jersey, landing at Newark Bay in 1665 by Howard Pyle, c. 1904–7. New Jersey Historical Society. Opposite above: Ivey Point, the Home of John Fenwick by William Patterson, c. 1850. Fenwick's home on the Delaware River was built in 1677. *Salem County Historical Society Opposite below: Johan Printz, governor of New Sweden from 1643–53. American Swedish Historical Museum, Philadelphia*

New Jersey thrived under British rule. Puritans and Quakers alike were attracted by promises of religious freedom, and farmers by the fertile, inexpensive land. Yet like colonists elsewhere along the Atlantic, New Jerseyans were torn between loyalty to the British king and thirst for independence. Soon after the 1776 signing of the Declaration of Independence, the colony found itself plunged into conflict. More than 100 battles were fought on New Jersey soil during the Revolutionary War, commencing with George Washington's 1776 rout of Hessian mercenaries on Christmas night at their Trenton encampment. Victories at Princeton the next month, and at Monmouth in June 1778—the longest sustained battle of the war—provided vital motivation for the rebels.

New Jersey was also the site of the war's gravest calamity. Encamped at

Left: Color engraving depicting the Battle of Monmouth in June 1778, with Molly Pitcher at the cannon. Molly Pitcher (actually Mrs. Mary Ludwig Hays) became an American legend when she followed her husband, John, into battle, carrying a pitcher of water to thirsty soldiers. When John fell wounded, Molly replaced him at the cannon. *Corbis-Bettman.* *Below:* Reenacting the Revolution. *Photo Kelly/Mooney* *Opposite: Washington Crossing the Delaware* by Emanuel Leutze, c. 1852. *The Metropolitan Museum of Art, New York*

Morristown starting in December 1779, Washington and nearly 12,000 troops endured the century's worst winter with meager supplies. Many were buried in their tents by blizzards. Relief came in the spring with the Marquis de Lafayette's troops. On April 14, 1783, the Continental Congress met in Princeton to sign the treaty giving the United States its independence. ❧

"WE HAVE NEVER EXPERIENCED A LIKE extremity at any period of the war."

> *George Washington in a 1779 letter to Governor George Clinton of New York, describing the grueling winter at Morristown*

Engraving of ships on the Passaic River in Newark, c. 1840s. With the arrival of the railroads in the 1830s, Newark grew into a thriving port city. Today the port is an important shipping hub for petroleum and general cargo.
Archive Photos

While lunching beside the Passaic River with General Washington, a young Revolutionary War colonel named Alexander Hamilton gazed up at Great Falls and imagined a modern factory town at its foot. He proposed as much to Congress in 1791, and New Jersey Governor William Paterson, seizing the opportunity, signed a charter for the Society for Useful Manufactures that year. A new town—Paterson, America's first planned industrial city—was plotted at the base of the falls.

Throughout the 19th century, Jersey City, Newark, Trenton, Camden, and especially Paterson grew dramatically, transforming the state's profile from agricultural to industrial. During the War of 1812, when British textile imports were cut off, Paterson's cotton mills helped keep Americans clothed. In the 1840s the mills converted to silk production and earned Paterson the nickname "Silk City." That city also was where Samuel Colt manufactured revolvers and where Thomas Rogers made the first locomotive. (During the Civil War, Paterson led the country in producing locomotives.) After the war, New Jersey's factories attracted workers from the rural South, as well as ever-increasing waves of immigrants from central and eastern Europe. 🐟

Great Falls on the Passaic River at Paterson. The Great Falls/S.U.M. (Society for Useful Manufactures) Historic District preserves parts of the old industrial area.
Photo Walter Choroszewski

"HAMILTON...RECOGNIZED THE GREAT FALLS OF THE PASSAIC as a site where would someday arise the world's most fruitful workshop. The tumbling stream...would, he thought, provide sufficient power to turn the wheels of every factory that the nation could ever build...."

Harry Emerson Wildes, Twin Rivers: The Raritan and the Passaic, *1943*

"Two minutes off this seething industrial highway...
New Jersey bursts open like a rose."

John Gunther, Inside U.S.A., 1947

The Garden State

Not long after Quakers established the first New Jersey farm in 1675, the green, fertile peninsula became known as the "garden of the world." The highland valleys of the north proved ideal for raising dairy cows and livestock; by 1879, locally made ice cream was a staple in New Jersey homes and ice-cream parlors. That same year, the state became the country's chicken capital. South Jersey's climate and soil yielded bumper crops of deciduous fruits, including winesap apples and many varieties of peaches. Bush fruits such as berries also grow abundantly, especially in the sandy soil of the Pine Barrens.

As the population shifted to the cities, the state's dominant form of agriculture became the small truck farm. In addition to superb tomatoes, blueberries, and peaches, New Jersey's nearly year-round bounty included—then as now—sweet Jersey corn, string beans, strawberries, beets, spinach, asparagus, squash, melons, and pumpkins.

The Jersey Tomato

Although today it's the state's single biggest crop, the tomato was greeted with suspicion and horror when it was first introduced, via South America and Florida, in the early 19th century. Folk wisdom held that the red fruit was either a poison or an aphrodisiac, but New Jersey judge Robert Gibbon Johnson argued to the contrary: to make his case, he ate an entire bushel at one sitting. By 1931, when the invention of tomato juice stepped up the demand, the state was growing a wide variety of hybrids including the renowned Rutgers "Jersey Tomato." Now trademarked, the designation refers to prescribed growing and packing methods, applied to several varieties that produce superior, vine-ripened fruit that nonetheless resist bruising.

Above: Maxwell House's neon sign was a north Jersey landmark for many years. *Right:* Window sign for Nabisco's Mickey Mouse Cookies. Founded in East Hanover in 1898, Nabisco pioneered the cardboard cracker carton lined with waxed paper. Previously, crackers had been sold out of cracker barrels on the floors of general stores. *Both, Robert Heide and John Gilman*

Growing food leads naturally to putting it up, and thanks to its strong manufacturing base, New Jersey had an edge over other farming states. Small wonder it was a pioneer in processing foods, from canning soup to bottling cranberry juice to freezing vegetables and fruits. Dozens of household names—including Ocean Spray (cranberry products), Snow's (frozen and canned seafood), Progresso (canned soup), My-T-Fine (pudding), and Maxwell House coffee (whose animated "Good to the Last Drop" sign was visible from western Manhattan)—got their start in New Jersey.

The forefather of them all was Charles F. Seabrook, who began his agricultural empire around 1900 with 57 acres of south-central farmland. In the 1930s, a Seabrook

employee named Clarence Birdseye (who later left for General Foods) developed a quick-freezing process that revolutionized the industry. By the time Seabrook Farms was sold in the 1960s, it was one of the largest agribusinesses in the world. ❦

M'm! M'm! Good!

Transformed into a cultural icon in the 1960s by pop artist Andy Warhol, Campbell's soup had been an American pantry staple for decades earlier. The Campbell Soup Company was founded in Camden in 1869 by fruit merchant Joseph Campbell—who once said that it all started with a red-ripe Jersey tomato—but it wasn't until 1897 that a young employee invented condensed soup in a tin, which dramatically cut packaging, shipping, and storage costs. The famous red-and-white label came along the following year, and in 1904 the cherubic Campbell Kids were introduced in trolley-car ads. Although the original soup plant was demolished in 1991, world headquarters remain in Camden—also home to the Campbell Museum, a showcase for the company's collection of soup tureens.

Advertisement from 1926 promotional booklet for Campbell's soup. Over the years, other Campbell giveaways have included salt and pepper shakers, mugs, cereal dishes, spoons, dolls, cookies, and recipe booklets. *Robert Heide and John Gilman*

Terra-cotta tile, manufactured in Perth Amboy in the 1930s, decorates the newly restored Paramount Theater and Convention Hall complex on the boardwalk in Asbury Park. *Photo John Gilman*

The slogan "Trenton makes, the world takes," on the railroad bridge across the Delaware River, once could have applied not just to Trenton but to a dozen New Jersey manufacturing cities. From the first Dutch copper mine, opened in the Kittatinny Mountains around 1640, through Thomas Edison's Menlo Park invention factory and well beyond, New Jersey has prided itself on its industries and its industriousness.

Some manufacturing towns grew up around a natural resource. Trenton's clay pits gave rise to a thriving pottery and tableware industry: Lenox china has been made here since 1889, Anchor Pottery is known for its distinctively glazed Stanglware, and the Trent Tile Company created terra-cotta tiles for skyscrapers and apartment houses. In south Jersey, the native fine white sand was used by local glassmakers such as Kimble Glass Works in Vineland.

"BEFORE A JEWELER'S WINDOW IN VENICE'S PIAZZA San Marco, a New Jerseyan asked her husband, 'Buy me that ring—I want a souvenir to remind me of moonlit nights and gondoliers.' The husband asked the jeweler for a closer look and noted the stamp inside the ring: 'Made in Newark.'"

Old New Jersey tale

Above: Place setting in the historic "Autumn" pattern, from the Lenox Presidential Collection. Designed by Frank Graham Holmes, the firm's chief designer from 1905 to 1954, and introduced in 1919, this finely detailed china is made in Pomona. The first American-made china used in the White House was designed by Holmes for President Wilson in 1918; Lenox services were also made for Presidents Roosevelt and Truman. *Courtesy Lenox, Inc. Left:* Master cutter at the Waterford plant in Wall Township. *New Jersey Newsphotos*

Other industries arose from forestry, mining, and manufacture. Newark's status as a transportation hub made nearby Irvington the logical site for the Lionel Train Corporation from 1915 through the 1970s. The Singer Sewing Machine Company was founded in Elizabeth in 1873; so were companies producing refined petroleum, beds, soap, clothing, furniture, and steel machinery. Jersey City's Joseph Dixon Crucible Company was a school-supply mecca for decades, producing pencils, crayons, erasers, and pencil boxes emblazoned with cartoon characters. ❧

Left: Lionel Electric Trains advertisement, c. 1926. A special Mickey Mouse handcar produced by Lionel in Irvington in the depths of the Great Depression sold for $1 each and saved the company from bankruptcy. *Lionel, L.L.C. Below:* Popeye with punching bag wind-up toy, c. 1945, made by the J. Chein Company of Newark. *New Jersey Newsphotos*

Industry Redefined

Today, though traditional industries still thrive in New Jersey, the state is more closely associated with pharmaceuticals—in whose production New Jersey leads the nation—research science, and high technology. Bell Labs, with headquarters in Murray Hill, Union, and Holmdel, is perhaps the state's most prominent corporate research firm; here a pair of scientists recorded the echo of the original Big Bang, a feat that won them the Nobel Prize for physics in 1978. For decades, Princeton's Institute for Advanced Study has nurtured scientists; during the 1940s and 50s, Albert Einstein was often spotted here, riding the campus paths on his bicycle. And clustered along Route 1 between New Brunswick and Princeton are so many high-tech companies, large and small, that the area has been dubbed the Silicon Valley of the East.

Right: **Charles Lindbergh and the "Spirit of St. Louis" at Newark Airport, c. late 1920s.** *Newark Public Library* *Below:* **Label from Jersey Central brand fine-cut tobacco, c. 1870s.** *Private collection. Opposite:* **A freighter being launched at the Federal Shipbuilding Company's dockyard in Kearny, 1932.** *Newark Public Library*

From the first experimental "steam waggon," demonstrated in Hoboken in 1824, New Jersey has held a key place in railroad history. The nation's first railroad charter was given in 1830 to the Camden and Amboy, which linked Philadelphia with New York. By the 1920s train service ran to all the Jersey shore towns, and the Erie-Lackawanna and Jersey Central helped develop the north Jersey Lakelands. Paterson's locomotive industry helped make the state a

railroad nexus. Although rail traffic is now much reduced, New Jersey's 112 stations—60 of them historic landmarks—testify to an era of pell-mell growth and architectural invention.

New Jersey pioneered in water and air travel as well. The state has deep water ports on both sides: at Camden and Trenton on the Delaware and at Newark, Elizabeth, and Bayonne on the Hudson River and New York Bay. John Fitch of Trenton launched the world's first operating steamboat on the Delaware River in 1786, and the first successful submarine was tested in 1881 in the Passaic River. The world's first ferry service, between Hoboken and Manhattan, began in 1811; the Delaware and Raritan Canal, chartered in 1830, became one of the country's three chief canals. The word "airport" was coined here in 1919, when the world's first municipal airport opened in Atlantic City. Many aircraft plants operated in the state, including Wright Aeronautical Corporation in Paterson, manufacturer of Lindbergh's "Spirit of St. Louis" engine. ❧

Jersey Transportation Landmarks

World's first ferry service, 1811

First operating railroad in America, Hoboken, 1825

Morris Canal, 1831

Camden and Amboy RR linked Philadelphia with New York, 1840

Locomotives, Lindbergh's airplane engine built in Paterson

Newark Airport, one of nation's busiest, opened 1928

Hiya, Hon:
Jersey Diner Lingo

Jersey diner servers speak a language all their own when they're relaying your order to the grill cook. Here's a sampling from this unique lexicon.

Flop Two: *two fried eggs, turned over*

Hot One: *bowl of chili*

Wimpy: *hamburger (from the burger-loving character in the comic strip "Popeye")*

Life Preserver: *doughnut*

Hoboken Special: *pineapple soda with chocolate ice cream*

Roadside diners can be found in virtually every state, but nowhere are they so numerous as in New Jersey. The state boasts more than 600 of them, many open 24 hours a day and some the sole survivors of Depression-era chains that favored "white" in their names: White Rose, White Diamond, White Tower, and White Manna. Derived from horse-drawn lunch wagons of the 1890s, diners took root after the turn of the century, when used and abandoned trolleys, electric streetcars, and railroad dining cars were refurbished and moved to busy neighborhoods. Aficionados still seek out early specimens with wood-paneled interiors or in the "Streamline" style with stainless steel, glass blocks, and blue or peach mirrors. In the mid-20th century, diners were manufactured by the dozens by local companies such as the Jerry O'Mahoney Company and Kullman Industries. Today, Kullman is producing new 1950s-style "Blue Comet" diners with clean, curvilinear stainless-steel exteriors and chromium and glass-brick detail. Wherever you find it, the Jersey diner is still a great place for cheap American fare such as hamburgers, french fries, and Jersey fresh eggs in a skillet. ❧

Above: Unchanged since the late 1920s, the Summit Diner continues in business across the road from the Summit railroad station. *Photo Walter Choroszewski Opposite: Tick Tock Diner by John Baeder, 1983. Courtesy the artist*

Diner Day Trips

Harris Diner, East Orange Built in 1952 and still 100% original, serves the "out-of-this-world" Dagwood Sputnik

Max's Grill, Harrison Built in 1929, now serves Spanish-Portuguese food

Miss America Diner, Jersey City Streamline style, built in the 1950s

Short Stop Diner, Bloomfield 1950s chrome and Formica, home of the He-Man Cheese Omelette

Summit Diner, Summit Opened in 1929; Ernest Hemingway is said to have loved the gigantic BLTs

White Mana in Jersey City, White Manna in Hackensack Both made their debuts at the 1939 New York World's Fair

> *"Genius is one percent inspiration and ninety-nine percent perspiration."*
>
> Thomas Alva Edison, Life, 1932

Thomas Edison and his son in front of Glenmont. Now part of the Edison National Historic Site in West Orange, the Edison home occupies a 15.5-acre estate and contains its original furnishings, including Edison's "thought bench."
Library of Congress

Born in Ohio, the largely self-taught Thomas Alva Edison (1847–1931) chose New Jersey as the place to pursue his dreams of invention. It was one of history's happiest relocations. First in a Newark manufacturing plant and later in his "invention factory" on a hill in Menlo Park, Edison developed scores of new products that would transform the way people communicated, illuminated their homes and streets, and spent their leisure hours. His first invention was an electric vote recorder; after he

Left: *Annabelle Butterfly Dance* by W. K. L. Dickson and William Heise, 1895. These hand-colored frames are enlargements from an early motion picture produced by the Edison Manufacturing Company. *Library of Congress. Below:* An Edison incandescent bulb, on display at the Laboratory Complex at the Edison NHS. Perhaps no invention so transformed the lives of so many people. *Photo Michael Melford*

developed the phonograph in 1879 he put it aside, regarding it as a toy with few practical applications. He was more perceptive about his incandescent electric light bulb, for which he filed a patent the same year; to make it affordable, he also invented the central generating station. Edison's other inventions include the motion-picture camera, an electric typewriter using revolving balls, and many improvements to the telegraph industry, where he had worked as a young man. Perhaps most significantly, the "Wizard of Menlo Park" established a new model for research, in which experimentation for its own sake was enthusiastically encouraged and failure was seen as a step along the path to success. ❧

"REMEMBER, NOTHING THAT'S GOOD WORKS BY ITSELF, JUST to please you. You've got to make the damn thing work."

Thomas Alva Edison, Life, 1932

S-Bend in an Elevated Section of the New Jersey Turnpike by Rackstraw Downes, 1996. Downes paints industrial scenes with a grandeur that renders them almost sublime. *Marlborough Gallery, Inc., New York Opposite: Holland Tunnel* by Lisbeth Firmin, 1999. This artist paints her urban subjects with just enough delineation to be recognized. *Courtesy the artist and Cameo Appearances, NY*

The art of getting from here to there has been a New Jersey preoccupation since at least 1664, when the Dutch built the colony's first paved road through Warren and Sussex counties. For much of the state's history, moving people efficiently to and from New York City was the primary objective—a goal that spawned many solutions and innovations. Once there were more than 75 covered wooden bridges in the state; today only one remains, eclipsed by the more than 6,000 conventional bridges crossing some 6,000 miles of rivers and tributaries. The nation's first toll "turnpike" was introduced here in 1801: with the turn of a pike stuck in the ground every 10 miles, travelers were granted right of

passage. Later firsts included the "Jersey Barrier" (a concrete divider down the middle of a highway), the traffic circle, and the cloverleaf system of on- and off-ramps. The modern bridge-and-tunnel era began in the 1920s with the construction of the Benjamin Franklin Bridge and the Holland Tunnel, which links New Jersey, Philadelphia, and New York City. ❧

Counting the cars on the New Jersey
  Turnpike
They've all come to look for America.

"America," words and music by Paul Simon, 1968

George Washington Bridge by Israel Litwak, c. 1940s. *Corbis. Opposite above:* A worker aloft on the Delaware Memorial Bridge. *Photo Kevin Fleming/Corbis Opposite below:* The New Jersey Turnpike connects the George Washington Bridge in the north with the Delaware Memorial Bridge in the south, with connections to the Pennsylvania Turnpike, and—over a 10-mile spur across the Jersey meadows—to the Holland Tunnel and lower Manhattan. *Photo Walter Choroszewski*

"Riding relaxes me. Especially the Turnpike."

Eddie Quinn, a fictional commissioner of the New Jersey Turnpike Authority,
in Dark Horse, *by Fletcher Knebel, 1972*

Highways and Skyways

An intricate tracery of bridges, tunnels, parkways, and expressways connects New Jersey to its mid-Atlantic neighbors. The 3,500-foot-long George Washington Bridge opened in 1931, a "symbol of cooperation between the colonial sister states of New Jersey and New York"; 1932 saw the completion of the 3.7-mile-long steel-and-concrete Pulaski Skyway, the most expensive engineering feat of its time. Asphalt fever arose again in the 1950s, when several great thoroughfares—including the New Jersey Turnpike, the Garden State Parkway, and the Palisades Interstate Parkway—enabled commuters and scenery-gazers alike to experience New Jersey from behind tinted windshields.

The New Jersey Turnpike

Thanks to poets, songwriters, and novelists, the New Jersey Turnpike is possibly the state's most celebrated—and castigated—landmark. The 133-mile toll road, officially U.S. 95, nearly bisects the state from the George Washington Bridge in the northeast to the Delaware Memorial Bridge in the southwest — a tour of the state's interior industrial belt. When it opened in 1952, it was the Miracle Turnpike, a road that could be traveled at speeds from 60 to 75 miles per hour in what its creators envisioned would be a state of soothing relaxation. Today it is seen primarily as a means for covering miles as quickly as possible, with occasional detours off the numbered exits or into the rest areas named for notable New Jerseyans.

Rest Areas on the Jersey Turnpike

All 13 rest areas are named for famous New Jerseyans or for Americans who made a contribution to history while living in New Jersey. The list reads south to north.

Clara Barton

John Fenwick

Walt Whitman

James Fenimore Cooper

Richard Stockton

Woodrow Wilson

Molly Pitcher

Joyce Kilmer

Thomas Edison

Grover Cleveland

William Halsey

Alexander Hamilton

Vince Lombardi

Six Scenic Scenes (Panel 2) by William Wegman, 1997. Installation at the Atlantic City Convention Center. Wegman poked gentle fun at New Jersey archetypes in this 5-by-25-foot photomural.
Courtesy the artist

Murals, monuments, and public sculpture abound in New Jersey, where popular art is taken both seriously and lightly. A scavenger hunt could be organized on the Founding Fathers theme—statues of George Washington are well-nigh ubiquitous, an elaborate bronze likeness of Peter Stuyvesant stands in Jersey City, and a bust and tablet mark the spot in Weehawken where Alexander Hamilton was killed in a duel with Aaron Burr.

No one need search for art at Princeton University; the beautiful campus is replete with outdoor sculpture from the John B. Putnam, Jr. Memorial Collection, including works by Alexander Calder, Jacques Lipchitz, Henry Moore, Louise Nevelson, George Segal, and Pablo Picasso. Another important gathering of outdoor art is found at Grounds for Sculpture in Hamilton, east of Trenton. This 22-acre park and museum, created by sculptor J. Seward Johnson, Jr. (artistic scion of the New Brunswick Johnson & Johnson family), features changing exhibits of contemporary sculpture in a serenely landscaped setting that once housed the New Jersey State Fair. And Atlantic City is home to a variety of recent works commissioned by the State Council on the Arts, from William Wegman's photomurals of New Jersey

archetypes to Jonathan Borofsky's whimsical flying fish suspended from the ceiling of the convention center. ❧

Above: Five Flying Fish *by Jonathan Borofsky, 1997.* New Jersey State Council on the Arts. *Left:* Déjeuner Déjà Vu *by J. Seward Johnson, Jr., 1994 Johnson's homage to the Manet masterpiece is installed at the Grounds for Sculpture Museum and Park in Hamilton, which also displays changing exhibits in the 22-acre park and 10,000-square-foot museum.* Grounds for Sculpture

THE ART OF POLITICS

Right: **Former Rhodes Scholar, professional basketball star, and New Jersey Senator Bill Bradley.** *Photo Wally McNamee/Corbis. Below:* **A 1912 political cartoon of Woodrow Wilson. Wilson's legacy lives on in Princeton University's Woodrow Wilson School of Public and International Affairs.** *Corbis-Bettman*

Thanks to 19th-century economic and political agendas and to a 1927 state constitutional amendment, New Jersey today is a welter of 566 counties, cities, towns, townships, boroughs, villages, and special districts—more governmental entities than any other state regardless of size.

Complicated as it seems, this patchwork reflects New Jersey's independent-minded character. Historically, the state's northern half has tended to vote Democratic, the southern half Republican, but a strong labor base has modulated both parties' politics toward the liberal end of the spectrum.

New Jersey has contributed notably in larger political arenas, too. Princeton and Rutgers in particular have given the state and nation a distinguished roster of statesmen and politicians—among them 11 New Jersey governors as well as U.S. Presidents James Madison, Grover Cleve-

July 13 1912   THE NEW RIDER   Price 10 Cents

land, and Woodrow Wilson. Wilson, who graduated from Princeton in 1879, went on to become the university's president and the state's governor. At this writing, former New Jersey Senator Bill Bradley, a 1965 Princeton graduate and one-time pro basketball star, is contending for the 2000 Democratic presidential nomination. And Republican Christine Todd Whitman—New Jersey's first female governor—has announced her year 2000 run for the U.S. Senate. Both seem likely to remain major players on the national stage. ❧

"CAMPAIGNING IN MIDDLESEX COUNTY, WHITMAN, who normally does not eat at campaign stops, shoveled in a plateful of kielbasa at the South River Polish American Club. Members of the club explained that no candidate who had come to eat the polish sausage, potatoes, and sauerkraut during a campaign had lost...."

Sandy McClure, Christie Whitman: For the People, A Political Biography, 1996

Caricature by Dave Woodman of Governor Christine Todd Whitman from *New Jersey Monthly* magazine, illustrating her article "The End of the Jersey Joke." "Yes, I've heard the jokes about bosses," Whitman writes. "...Yes, I've heard the jokes about the oil refineries....

And if you must know what exit I'm from, you're out of luck. I proudly claim the entire state of New Jersey as my home." *New Jersey Monthly*

Modest, functional dwellings, reflecting Dutch, Quaker, and Puritan lifestyles, characterized New Jersey for much of its history. The first inhabitants, the Lenape, occupied round or oval structures made of saplings bound at the top and covered with bark strips or bundles of grass, with a chimney hole in the roof. Early European settlers used similar shelters when they first arrived but quickly advanced to log cabins, introduced to New Jersey—and North America—by Finnish immigrants.

Dutch and English colonists brought their home-building traditions with

Above: **Steuben House in Riveredge, Bergen County.** *Photo Walter Choroszewski.* *Right:* **Ford Mansion, Morristown.** *Photo Michael Melford/ Wheeler Pictures.* **Steuben House was General Washington's headquarters in 1780; the Ford Mansion was his headquarters during the grim winter of 1779–80.**

them, the Dutch building in brick and stone and the English in wood. The Dutch even imported bricks from their homeland, using native sandstone and river mud as mortar. Their English counterparts often left their homes unpainted or simply whitewashed them. By the Revolutionary era, though, Georgian and Palladian architecture were popular, as evidenced by Colonel Jacob Ford's Morristown mansion—George Washington's headquarters during the war.

Planned suburban communities have a long tradition in New Jersey. Since 1854, Llewellyn Park, spectacularly located on the slope of Orange Mountain, has housed the well-off in extraordinary homes of many architectural styles, including Thomas Edison's Victorian mansion, Glenmont. And Urban Farms in Franklin Lakes provided distinctive, well-designed homes and shared recreational space for the middle class in the 1950s. ❧

The James Rose residence in Ridgewood. Rose, sometimes called the James Dean of landscape architecture, built his experimental home and garden in the 1950s. The small dwelling of cinder block, mahogany, and salvaged materials is surrounded by a gem of garden modernism, the whole considered one of the 20th century's most innovative home environments.
Photo Pieter Estersohn

Cottages and Castles

Nineteenth-century industrialists and financiers came
home to New Jersey estates of unrestrained grandios-
ity. Most were imitative of European mansions, such
as the 110-room Florham—a replica of the west wing
of Hampton Court Palace—built in Morristown for a
granddaughter of Cornelius Vanderbilt—or Blairs-
den, in Peapack, which sprawled over 2,000 acres and
featured white marble busts of Roman emperors.
More in the local vernacular is the Batsto Mansion,
deep in the Pine Barrens where a bog-iron industry
once prospered. The oldest part of the house dates back
to 1785, with many additions built between 1815 and
1878. In 1876 Joseph Wharton, known as "the Nickel
King," bought the property and added a Victorian
facade, a fire tower, and grand porches.

On the Jersey shore, Ocean Grove is a living museum of Victorian homes. Chartered by Methodists in 1869, the town today limits new building to styles within strict historic guidelines. Internationally renowned architect and Princeton professor Michael Graves takes a more playful approach to tradition with his postmodern residences, including a four-story renovation in Princeton with a neo–Dutch Renaissance facade.

"MORRISTOWN WAS A COMMUTING TOWN EVEN IN THE nineties [1890s]. The 4:15 p.m. train was known as the 'millionaires' express' and carried a club car (dues only $60 per year but you had to get in) with its own porter and green-cushioned wicker chairs."

Mac Griswold and Eleanor Weller,
The Golden Age of American Gardens, 1991

Historic Homes

Batsto Mansion and Village
Hammonton
(609) 561-3262

Dey Mansion
Wayne
(973) 696-1776

Drumthwacket
Princeton
(609) 683-0057

Ford Mansion, Wick House
Morristown National
Historical Park
(973) 539-2085

Steuben House
Riveredge
Dutch Colonial gem
(201) 487-1739

William Trent House
Trenton
(609) 989-3027

Walt Whitman House
The poet's home, Camden
(609) 964-5383

Generally temperate—19th-century boosters bragged that its climate was 12 degrees warmer than New York's—New Jersey experiences hot, muggy summers and, in places, heavy snows that can challenge the most dedicated gardener. Inventive and even spectacular private gardens nevertheless thrive here, some in natural settings, some in hothouses. Among the latter, none is more lavish than the 11 Victorian hothouse gardens of Duke estate near Somerville, created for tobacco heiress Doris Duke. They include a formal French garden, an Indo-Persian Garden resembling the Shalimar Gardens in Pakistan, an American Colonial garden, and—Duke's favorite—a tropical garden with rubber plants, orchids, and sago palm. The public can view these magical "gardens under glass" on regularly scheduled tours.

A few well-maintained estate gardens testify to Gilded Age extravagance, notably those at Drumthwacket in Princeton. Built in 1835 and long owned by Princeton University trustee Moses Taylor Pyne, the Greek Revival mansion is now the governor's residence. At the practical end of the spectrum is the Tempe Wick Garden in Morristown National Historical Park, originally the property of a prosperous Colonial farmer. Plantings include flax for weaving linen, soapwort for laundering, medicinal and kitchen herbs, and edible plants. Also of historic significance is Sunnybank, once the home of Albert Payson Terhune, author of *Lad, a Dog*. 🐝

"...POETRY ON SPRING AFTERNOONS in the gardens of the big estates near Princeton, while swans made effective atmosphere in the artificial pools, and low clouds sailed harmoniously above the willows."

F. Scott Fitzgerald, This Side of Paradise, 1920

Below: The gardens at Drumthwacket have undergone a recent restoration that complements their classic original design. *Opposite above:* The French Garden at Duke Gardens. *Both photos, Walter Choroszewski. Opposite below:* Tempe Wick Garden, maintained as an example of a working Colonial farm and household. *Photo Judy White/ New Leaf Images*

Down the Shore by Ann Cooper, 1999. Cooper composes her watercolor still-lifes around a group of objects that tell a story, usually against patterned backgrounds. *Courtesy the artist*

Within its tri-state area, New Jersey is a mecca for hunters of state-culture collectibles—trinkets and memorabilia with a specific (if long-forgotten) connection to a certain place and time in New Jersey history. Flea markets, street fairs, and antique shops can be gold mines for such collectors, and the state's many small museums—such as the New Jersey Historical Society in Newark and the Atlantic City Historical Museum—often feature Jerseyana in special exhibits. Among the most sought-after items are tablecloths from the 1940s and 1950s with detailed state maps; dime banks in the shape of Atlantic City's Convention Hall (originally constructed in 1929); original Monopoly board games; and vintage postcards from New Jersey towns and cities. If the prices seem steep to the casual collector, there are always modern-day memorabilia to be saved for posterity: Jersey Devil T-shirts; Asbury Park salt-and-pepper shakers; and ceramic tiles depicting the state bird, the eastern goldfinch. More conventional antiques, from furnishings to textiles, also draw browsers and buyers to fairs, the Lambertville flea market, and restored Colonial towns like Chester and Hopewell. 🐝

"HOOK'S 'SHARPER' HAD ARRIVED FROM TRENTON to purchase Mrs. Mortis's quaint and beautiful quilts....he had discovered that in this age there existed a hungry market for anything—trivets, samplers, whalebone swifts, buttonhooks, dragware, Staffordshire hens...savouring of an older America."

John Updike, The Poorhouse Fair, *1958*

Above: **Milbern State Plate for New Jersey, Popegossler china by Steubenville, c. 1938.** The state capitol and other landmarks are depicted, along with the ill-fated zeppelin *Hindenberg. Left:* Tinted postcard of a Sunday bathing party at Atlantic City, c. 1910. *Both, Robert Heide and John Gilman*

Billy's Chicken Savoy

Along with some of Jersey's best deep-dish pizza, the legendary Reservoir Pizzeria and Restaurant in South Orange prepares this tangy dish.

One whole chicken,
  hacked into small pieces
1 cup olive oil
1 cup flour
2 cups freshly grated Parmesan
  cheese
¼ cup dried oregano
¼ tsp. salt
¼ tsp. black pepper
5 garlic cloves, minced
¾ cup red wine vinegar
¼ cup balsamic vinegar
½ cup chicken stock, heated

Roll chicken pieces in heated olive oil (reserve 3–4 tbsp. oil for frying), then in flour, then in a mixture of oregano, salt, pepper, and 1 cup cheese. Fry in a large cast iron or stainless sauté pan over medium-high heat, turning often. Combine garlic and vinegar, heat briefly. Drain oil from pan, add vinegar mixture, heat just to boiling. Put pan with chicken under broiler 1–2 minutes, turning pieces. Toss with 1 cup cheese and the stock, sprinkle with more pepper, and serve.

Ethnic diversity, a farming heritage, and aquatic abundance make dining in New Jersey an exuberantly eclectic experience. Within the mile-square Ironbound district of Newark the diner can sample authentic Spanish and Portuguese fare such as paella, rabbit stew, and mariscada (a garlicky seafood stew). Up the hill, in the Italian First Ward, are establishments that have sold home-made macaroni and fancy Old World pastries since the late 19th century. Outside Lakewood, in the Pine Barrens, is the old White Russian enclave of Rova Farms, where a sprawling restaurant offers pelmeni and borscht with cold vodka. Union City is home to numerous Cuban and Ecuadorian restaurants, while the small township of Union boasts two German butcher shops.

You can't beat New Jersey for classic American fare, either. Roadside diners claim unique versions of hamburgers, pizza, and chicken, while seafood restaurants along the shore serve whole steamed lobsters, clampots, fried shrimp, and broiled scallops. Saltwater taffy was invented here—according to legend, after a high tide bathed a vendor's confections in brine. ☙

Above: Pastrami sandwich at Jack Coopers in Edison. *New Jersey Newsphotos. Left:* Waxed-paper wrapper for Shriver's famous salt water taffy. *Robert Helde and John Gilman. Opposite:* Owner and chef Branco Raiac of the Villa Romagna Restaurant in Clifton. *Photo Erik Rank*

High Summer by Alice Steer Wilson, 1993. Wilson has been painting scenes of Cape May since the 1960s. *Courtesy the artist. Opposite above:* Souvenir fan from Shark River Hills. *Robert Heide and John Gilman. Opposite below:* Funtown Pier, Seaside Heights. *Photo Scott Barrow*

By the Beautiful Sea

Stretching for 127 miles along shoals that separate the ocean from a series of lagoons and bays, the Jersey Shore offers delights for every sort of pleasure-seeker. For swimming and boardwalk strolling, more than 50 shore towns beckon, from Sea Bright to the white sands of Point Pleasant. For nature lovers, there's Sandy Hook—part of the Gateway National Recreation Area, a seven-mile-long peninsula that shelters 270 species of birds in its dune, marsh, estuary, and beach habitats—and farther south, Island Beach State Park, with over 3,000 acres of nature trails. Architecture buffs can admire the 19th-century Victorians of Deal, Spring Lake, and Ocean Grove, while fans of funkier amusements can stroll the famed boardwalks of Atlantic City, Seaside Heights, and Wildwood.

The history of the Jersey Shore as a pleasure-ground began in the early 1800s. Cape May was the first fashionable resort; during the 1850 season, 17,000 visitors summered there, mostly well-to-do types from New York, Philadelphia, and Baltimore. Improved rail travel opened the shore to a more democratic tourist class. By the 1880s, the train trip from Philadelphia took only a day, enabling thousands of middle-class folk to enjoy beach vacations.

"THE SURF LUBRICATES THE JOINTS LIKE OIL.... THE long waves gently shock the frame and stir the sluggish blood into fresher motion....Grave men fling out their limbs like colts in pasture; dignified women... sport like girls at recess.... Young men and maidens forget how far society keeps them apart and together dash in, in entire forgetfulness of all society may think."

A visitor to Ocean Grove in 1874

The Jersey Devil Cocktail

A specialty of the Oyster Creek Inn at Leeds Point on Great Bay, this powerful concoction is named after the official state demon.

1 shot applejack
1 shot rum
2 shots cranberry-juice cocktail

Shake with ice and pour into a tall stemmed glass.

NATIONAL BEAUTY TOURNAMENT
BATHERS REVUE   ROLLING CHAIR PARADE
SEPT. 5·6·7. 1923

Poster for 1923 Atlantic City Pageant. Atlantic City kicked off the Jazz Age with a winning promotion: a bathing beauty "mermaid" contest that became the Miss America pageant. *Archive Photos*

Atlantic City is famous as the only place outside Nevada where virtually all forms of gambling are legal; its glittering casinos beside the great boardwalk draw millions of serious and recreational players. But by the time gambling was legalized in 1976, the city had been targeting the tourist dollar for more than a century. Atlantic City was incorporated in 1854, with 21 voting citizens; the first train from Camden arrived later that year, bringing 600 visitors to a still-unfinished hotel. By 1859 a building boom had produced 130 structures, including three churches, a schoolhouse, a market, and a lighthouse. The world's first boardwalk was completed in 1870, the first amusement pier in 1882. Two years later the rolling chair was invented here, begetting a unique fleet of human-powered sightseeing conveyances still in operation today.

Besides the piers, casinos, and shops, two attractions have certified Atlantic City's place in American history. The game of Monopoly, invented in 1933 by a visiting

Pennsylvanian, memorializes the city's streets and railroads while inviting players to indulge in real-estate fever. And the annual Miss America pageant, held here since 1921, unites pomp and kitsch in a style imitated by hundreds of lesser contests around the world. ❧

"IT IS AN ENDLESS DRESS PARADE...IN WHICH everybody is one of the reviewers as well as one of the reviewed. The animation, the overflowing good nature, the laughter and contagious hilarity of the restless throng is irresistible....Nowhere in the world is there such a kaleidoscope of beauty!"

An Atlantic City native son on the famed boardwalk, 1904

Above: **Taj Mahal casino, Atlantic City.** *Photo Bill Mitchell/Archive Photos*
Left: Miss America Float by Malcah Zeldis, 1989. A Boardwalk parade has long been a Miss America pageant tradition. *The Noyes Museum of Art, Oceanville, New Jersey*

Right: The New Jersey Devils celebrate after winning the Stanley Cup at the Meadowlands Arena in East Rutherford. The Meadowlands site was diked to protect it from flooding; its four freshwater lagoons have become habitats for migratory birds, egrets, and wild swans. *New Jersey Newsphotos.* Below: Giants Stadium. *New Jersey Newsphotos*

Athletics, both amateur and professional, have long captivated New Jersey's imagination. It was in Hoboken, on June 19, 1846, that the first "open challenge" baseball game in the world was played, 23 years before the professional sport was founded. (For the record, the New York Club beat the Knickerbockers.) Although the state hosts no major league ball club, Little League is a big-ticket attraction in many communities: the 1998 Little League World Series championship was won by a home team, Toms River East.

No development transformed local sporting life more than the 750-acre Meadowlands Sports Complex, which opened in 1976 in a once-vast tract of swamps and meadows near the Hackensack River in Bergen County. The complex's racetrack, arena, and stadium draw nearly 10 million patrons yearly to thoroughbred and harness horse racing, and professional sports galore. New Jersey fans have an edge on New York because both of New York's NFL football squads the Giants and the Jets— play here. Meadowlands also hosts home games of the NBA's New Jersey Nets and pro hockey's New Jersey Devils, as well as boxing matches, concerts, and circuses. ✥

Far Hills Race Day is an annual event benefitting a local hospital; horses compete in steeplechase and turf races. *Photo Scott Barrow*

"ONE AFTERNOON DURING A PRESEASON PICKUP GAME [AT Princeton], a mustached man wearing cut-off khaki shorts... asked to join the workout, in an accent I mistook as Scottish.... The tall stranger got an elbow and returned one; then he took a pass, swept across the lane, and hit a fifteen-foot hook shot....'Couldn't be Scottish,' I thought. He said, 'Belz the name, basketball the game, and South Jersey is my home'."

Bill Bradley, on his first meeting with Princeton basketball great Carl Belz, 1996

Belters and Crooners

From swing and jazz through rock and rap, New Jersey has produced an astonishing share of famous musicians. A musical Who's Who includes Dionne Warwick and her niece Whitney Houston, artists of the pop standard; Lauryn Hill and Queen Latifah, rising stars of hip-hop and rap; jazz singer Sarah Vaughan; big-band leader Count Basie; pop stylist Connie Francis; and versatile singer-songwriter Paul Simon.

Most closely associated with their native state are two vastly different yet equally charismatic singers, Frank Sinatra and Bruce Springsteen. Born to Italian immigrants in Hoboken in 1915, Sinatra became "the Voice" of the Harry James and Tommy Dorsey big bands, making bobby-soxers swoon with his seamless baritone and intense delivery. His transformation in the 1950s from swing to swingin' was just as dramatic.

Above: **Bruce Spring-steen.** *Photo Michael S. Yamashita.* **Right:** **Frank Sinatra.** *Photo Herman Leonard/StageImage*

Before the music ends,
I must go to Hoboken
One more time.
I want to run down the streets
Where that thin Italian kid ran....

"Before the Music Ends," words and music by Gordon Jenkins, sung by Frank Sinatra, 1980

Freehold native Bruce Springsteen's first album, released in 1972, was *Greetings from Asbury Park*; the cover depicted a postcard of the seaside resort in its heyday. Singing of beer joints, bikers, and lonely Jersey girls, Springsteen assured audiences at Asbury Park's Stone Pony that "down at the shore everything's all right." He catapulted from local renown to international stardom in the 1980s, earning the nickname "The Boss" for his explosive energy and commanding presence.

Beyond the Palace hemi-powered
   drones scream down the boulevard
The girls comb their hair in
   rearview mirrors
And the boys try to look so hard
The amusement park rises bold and stark
Kids are huddled on the beach in a mist
I wanna die with you Wendy on the streets
   tonight
In an everlasting kiss

Bruce Springsteen, "Born to Run"

Above: Sarah Vaughan in 1955. *Photo Herman Leonard/Stagemage. Left:* Connie Francis, nicknamed "the empress of New Jersey," rocketed to fame with pop hits "Who's Sorry Now?," "Where the Boys Are," and "Lipstick on Your Collar." *Neal Peters Collection*

Singin' in the Rain at the Papermill Playhouse. This company presents everything from Rudolf Friml operettas to Stephen Sondheim productions; the building is beautifully set in a nature preserve. *Paper Mill Playhouse. Below:* Marlon Brando in *On the Waterfront. Robert Heide and John Gilman. Opposite:* Still from *Atlantic City. Photofest*

Living in the shadow of New York's Great White Way would give most states a theatrical inferiority complex, but New Jersey has its own proud stage tradition. The Papermill Playhouse in Millburn, New Jersey's official state theater since 1972, is a musical-theater showcase; Princeton's McCarter Theater won a Tony Award in 1994 as America's outstanding regional theater company. The New Jersey Shakespeare Festival presents classic and modern plays in the technologically sophisticated F. M. Kirby Shakespeare Theater on the campus of Drew University in Madison. New Brunswick is home to the Crossroads Theater Company, the nation's preeminent African-American theatrical organization.

As for the silver screen, New Jersey was the original Hollywood. The first movie studio was Thomas Edison's West Orange laboratory, and competitors were soon drawn to the area. The first feature-length film, *The Great Train Robbery,* was made in Caldwell in 1903; later in the decade, Fort Lee would be known as "the movie capital of the world." More recently, independent filmmakers such as Todd Solondz (*Welcome to the Dollhouse, Happiness*) and Kevin Smith (*Chasing Amy, Clerks*) have used New Jersey locations to potent effect in their low-budget, off-center productions. ❧

New Jersey Filmography

Three Little Girls in Blue Set in turn-of-the-century Atlantic City, this 1946 musical featured native daughters Celeste Holm and Vivian Blaine plus the song "On the Boardwalk."

On the Waterfront Shot in Hoboken, Elia Kazan's 1954 drama about harbor unions won eight Oscars.

The Miracle Worker Story of Helen Keller and her teacher, Annie Sullivan, starred Patty Duke and Anne Bancroft; shot in Newark.

Marjoe Oscar-winning 1972 documentary about fake evangelist Marjoe Gortner.

Atlantic City Burt Lancaster and Susan Sarandon in Louis Malle's 1980 drama about the impact of the casinos.

Friday the 13th The first of the sensational horror series (1980) was filmed at Camp NoBeBoSco.

Return of the Secaucus Seven John Sayles's low-budget character study of former college radicals.

Stardust Memories Woody Allen's 1980 seriocomic examination of fame was shot in Ocean Grove.

Cop Land 1997 drama about corrupt New York City cops who live across the river starred Sylvester Stallone, Robert De Niro, Harvey Keitel, and a host of New Jersey locations.

Orson Welles, actor and producer of the dramas broadcast by the Mercury Theatre Players.
Archive Photos

New Jersey sometimes seems a magnet for oversized debacles that generate oversized headlines. A glut of such disasters occurred in the 1920s and 30s, beginning in 1928 when Emilio Carranza, the Mexican aviator, crashed into the Pine Barrens while attempting a nonstop New York–Mexico City flight. In 1932, another famed pilot, Charles Lindbergh, endured a media maelstrom when his infant son was kidnapped from the Lindbergh estate near Hopewell and later murdered.

In September 1934, as horrified spectators watched from Asbury Park, a fire engulfed and sank the *Morro Castle,* recently returned from a vacation cruise to Cuba. That tragedy was dwarfed in 1937 by the dramatic midair explosion of the German zeppelin *Hindenburg* just yards above its landing pad in Lakehurst. After all this, it was no wonder that thousands of Americans were taken in by an October 30, 1938, "news bulletin" announcing the landing of a Martian spacecraft near Grovers Mill, New Jersey. The broadcast was part of a radio play produced by Orson Welles and John Houseman, adapted from H. G. Wells's *War of the Worlds.* 🌺

"This is one of the worst catastrophes in the world. Oh, the humanity…it's burst into flames… oh, my, this is terrible."

Radio broadcaster Herbert Morrison, covering the Hindenburg *explosion*

"THE FLASH IN THE SKY WAS VISIBLE within a radius of several hundred miles and the noise of the impact was heard as far north as Elizabeth."

From the radio play War of the Worlds

Above: News headlines of Lindbergh kidnapping. *The New Jersey Historical Society. Left:* The zeppelin *Hindenburg* explodes over New Jersey, 1937. *Archive Photos*

Above: **Stephen Crane.** *Photographer unknown. Archive Photos. Right: Allen Ginsberg Thumb-print Portrait by Hoop, 1997.* A true New Jersey visionary, Hoop (born Stephen Hooper) embarked in 1996 on his project of finger-printing the famous, then making color silkscreens from the prints, a tongue-in-cheek defense of civil liberties. *Robert Heide and John Gilman*

Since early statehood days, New Jersey has nurtured celebrated writers. Some—like critics Alexander Woollcott and Edmund Wilson and novelists Stephen Crane, Philip Roth, and Norman Mailer—made their careers in New York or abroad; others, like the poet Walt Whitman, chose New Jersey as a writing refuge. James Fenimore Cooper (1789–1851), considered America's first major novelist, based his Indian characters on observations of New Jersey's Lenape people. The poet Joyce Kilmer, born in New Brunswick in 1886, is best known for a single 12-line verse, "Trees." The most renowned Jersey bard is William Carlos Williams, the Rutherford pediatrician who crafted some of the century's finest prose and poetry, including a five-volume epic poem, *Paterson,* named for both the city and the historical figure.

Princeton University has long been a literary center in its own right, attracting students and teachers such as Philip

Freneau, poet of the Revolution; the German-born novelist Thomas Mann; and the prolific fiction writer Joyce Carol Oates. Pulitzer Prize–winning journalist and essayist John McPhee, author of *The Pine Barrens* and many other nonfiction works, was educated at Princeton and is now a professor there. ❧

"IF YOU'RE FROM NEW JERSEY," NATHAN HAD SAID, "and you write thirty books, and you win the Nobel Prize, and you live to be white-haired and ninety-five, it's highly unlikely but not impossible that after your death they'll decide to name a rest stop for you on the Jersey Turnpike. And so, long after you're gone, you may indeed be remembered but mostly by small children, in the backs of cars, when they lean forward and tell their parents, 'Stop, please, stop at Zuckerman— I have to make a pee.' For a New Jersey novelist that's as much immortality as it's realistic to hope for."

Philip Roth, The Counterlife, *1986*

Author and poet William Carlos Williams was born and lived in Rutherford, where he practiced pediatric medicine from 1910 to 1952, his home on Ridge Road, where he wrote and practiced, is on the National Register of Historic Places. Williams used Rutherford as Thoreau used Concord: as a specific setting that could yield universal truths. The town's public library contains first editions of his works and other memorabilia. *Archive Photos*

> Thought clambers up,
> snail like, upon the wet rocks
> hidden from sun and sight—
>   hedged in by the pouring torrent—
> and has its birth and death there
> in that moist chamber, shut from
> the world—and unknown to the world,
> cloaks itself in mystery—

William Carlos Williams, Paterson, Book I, *1946*

When English-born illustrators Harry Fenn and Charles Parsons settled there in the 1860s, Montclair, in picturesque Essex County, was a rural village of 2,000. That changed with the advent of the railroad in 1873—and with the arrival of George Inness in 1878. Inness, among the greatest American landscape painters of his time, had grown up in nearby Newark and was attracted to Montclair's diverse vistas: the Hudson River and Manhattan to the east, First Watchung Mountain to the west. By the 1890s, the "Inness colony" was a year-round artists' community whose residents included the sculptor Jonathan Scott Hartley, the portrait painter Douglas Volk, and the husband-and-wife team of Emilie Koehler Greenough and Walter Conant Greenough, who between them painted landscapes, created stained-glass windows, and designed book covers.

Unlike most 19th-century art colonies, Montclair thrives to this day—home to hundreds of visual artists, the nationally respected Montclair Art Museum, and many performing arts groups. So widespread is the city's reputation that recent school benefits and community concerts have attracted the likes of tap dancer Savion Glover and musicians Yo-Yo Ma, Emmanuel Ax, and Isaac Stern. ❧

"IS IT THAT WE CREATIVE TYPES ARE complicated souls who need to be inches away from the pulse of New York to feel alive? Or that we want to be in a place bucolic enough for those times when we need peace and quiet to create, and wish we were living on a farm?"

Painter and Montclair resident Rochelle Rubin, 1997

Above: Fox Leaf by Vivian McDuffie, 1995. McDuffie is the founder of Women Artists of Montclair. *Left: Early Autumn, Montclair* by George Inness, 1888. Once closely associated with the Hudson River School, Inness later favored a looser style influenced by the French Barbizon artists, as in this work. *Opposite: Snake Hill on the Jersey Meadows* by Charles Parsons, 1871. Although he worked mainly as an illustrator at *Harper's* magazine, Parson's passion was for water-colors. *All, The Montclair Art Museum*

Factories in New Jersey by Paul Weingarten, 1993. *Salander-O'Reilly Galleries, New York. Opposite above: Spiral, Jersey City* by Valeri Larko, 1998. In her close yet uncritical observations of industrial artifacts, Larko transforms this human-generated chaos into an acceptable echo of the natural world. *Courtesy the artist. Opposite below: West of Routes 1 & 9* by Tim Daly, 1986. Daly, a Hoboken artist, creates dark, moody paintings that imbue the industrial landscape with mystery through their use of muted light, shadow, and detail. *Courtesy the artist*

Painters and sculptors have found in New Jersey's concrete and steel cityscapes a stimulus for awe and admiration, irony and despair. Early in the 20th century, painters such as John Marin were thrilled by the sheer energy of buildings and bridges. Marin, born in Rutherford in 1870 and much influenced by the French avant-garde and by Chinese landscape painting, brought a giddy exuberance to his oils and watercolors of Manhattan, the Brooklyn Bridge, and the industrial landscape of Weehawken. A contemporary painter, Valeri Larko, also finds sensual pleasure in the built environment. Working on-site in the industrial parks of northern New Jersey, Larko creates large, vividly colored compositions that capture the paradoxical beauty of steel and rust.

Other artists have explored industry's darker side. Photographer George Tice's *Paterson* and *A New Jersey Portrait* document a desolate urban landscape, and Paul Weingarten's large oil paintings of Newark and Hoboken use grim manmade structures as a counterpoint to the prevailing forces of nature, sunsets, clouds, and wind. ❦

The Black Chair by Robert Birmelin, 1994. This painting may be hung with either end up. *Hackett-Freedman Gallery, San Francisco*

New Jersey is experiencing exciting ferment in the visual arts. Artists are moving into former factories in cities such as Hoboken, Jersey City, Newark, and Paterson, and provocative work by local artists is appearing in corporate showrooms, galleries, and important museums such as the New Jersey State Museum in Trenton, the Montclair Art Museum, the Newark Museum, and the Atlantic City Art Center. The state's arts renaissance began with Pop, Op, and minimalist art in the 1960s. Englewood resident Richard Anuskiewicz was heralded by *Life* magazine in 1965 as one of the new wizards of Op art; his dazzling paintings were more in demand than Jackson Pollock's. New Brunswick native George Segal's white figures, exhibited all over the state, have been called "plaster Pop," but their melancholy isolation belies the vivid brightness usually associated with the genre.

Left: *A Square of the Gap* by Barbara Kulicke, 1997. *Courtesy the artist.* Below: *Four + Fore=?* by Hoop, 1998. This piece was part of a 1998 exhibit, "Strokes of Genius." His eccentric use of automobiles has earned Hoop (who is also a performance artist) widespread press attention and two top awards in *Car & Driver* magazine's Best Car Installation contests. *Photo Robert Heide and John Gilman*

Today, New Jersey's contemporary art scene is epitomized at one extreme by Hoop, a Dadaesque conceptualist who has created a series of eccentric vehicles festooned variously with clocks, vinyl records, and fur. At the other extreme is muralist Barbara Kulicke, whose luminous work returns repeatedly to the Delaware Water Gap, rendering the countryside as a black silhouette against a deep blue sky—"the edge of the world against infinity," as Kulicke puts it. ❧

Lucy the Elevated Elephant

A beloved icon of American roadside architecture, Lucy was built in 1881 by a Philadelphia developer to attract investment to the then-new Atlantic City suburb of Margate. Today the ponderous pachyderm is a National Historic Landmark; visitors climb spiral staircases inside her legs for a view from the howdah on her back. Lucy's vital stats: height, 65 feet;

torso, 80 feet around; ears, 17 feet; tusks, 22 feet; and tail, 26 feet.

His Master's Voice

The figure of a seated black-and-white terrier, one ear cocked toward a gramophone horn, was trademarked in 1901 by Eldridge Johnson, founder of the Victor Talking Machine in Camden. Among the best-known images in advertising, "Little Nipper" has been incarnated in many forms, but most impressively in four stained-glass windows created in 1915 by Nicola D'Asenzo for RCA Victor's Camden headquarters.

Walking the Walk

"Boardwalk" is synonymous with Atlantic City, and the venerable shoreline promenade today offers diversions for all. Take a break from the casinos and shops to check out the Art Center and Historical Museum on Garden Pier, Ripley's Believe It or Not! Museum, and the rides on famed Steel Pier. The 1929 Convention Hall, site of the Miss America pageant, has been recently restored and boasts the world's largest pipe organ.

Cowtown Rodeo

You needn't go farther west than Woodstown to take in an authentic professional rodeo, complete with bull riding, team roping, and barrel racing. This part of southwestern New Jersey, near Vineland, was long known as the "cow capital of the first frontier," and the Cowtown Rodeo has been presented by the Harris family since 1929 (except during World War II). Current owner-producer Grant Harris is himself a champion rodeo rider. The show goes on Saturdays all summer long.

Fairytale Funhouse

Drivers tend to hit their brakes at the first sight of Hamburg's Gingerbread Castle, a Rhineland-cum-Disneyland fantasy where everyone gets to be a kid again. A story-loving businessman hired Florenz Ziegfeld's stage designer, Joseph Urban, to design the castle in 1930, and generations since have seen the classic tales come to life as local youngsters enact "Hansel and Gretel" and point out Humpty Dumpty, the witch's kitchen, and the gingerbread cookies and peppermint sticks embedded in the walls.

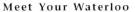

Meet Your Waterloo

Waterloo Village, a superb re-creation of an 18th-century village, is located in Allamuchy State Park near Stanhope. This National Historic Site encompasses 28 colonial structures and a Lenape village; May through October, the village hosts the Waterloo Festival of the Arts, presenting classical and popular music in a sylvan setting.

Great People

A selective listing of native New Jerseyans, focusing on the arts.

Meryl Streep (b. 1949), actress

William A. (Bud) Abbott (1896–1974) and **Louis Francis (Lou) Costello** (1908–1959), comedy team whose career spanned vaudeville, radio, TV, and movies

Edwin (Buzz) Aldrin (b. 1930), Apollo astronaut

Amiri Baraka (b. 1934), playwright, poet, and political activist; born LeRoi Jones

William (Count) Basie (1904–1984), jazz pianist, composer, and big-band leader

Moe Berg (1902–1972), baseball player and linguist turned American spy

Elias Boudinot (1740–1821), president of the Continental Congress (1782–83)

Grover Cleveland (1837–1908), 22nd and 24th president of the United States; only native son to become president

James Fenimore Cooper (1789–1851), known for his *Leatherstocking Tales;* considered first major novelist of the New World

Stephen Crane (1871–1900), novelist, best known for *The Red Badge of Courage*

Malcolm Forbes (1919–1990), publisher of *Forbes* magazine

Allen Ginsberg (1926–1997), poet and seminal figure of the "Beat Generation"

Joyce Kilmer (1886–1918), poet and literary critic best known for poem "Trees"

Dorothy Kirsten (1917–1992), operatic soprano

Jerry Lewis (b. 1926), comedian and movie actor

Norman Mailer (b. 1923), novelist and nonfiction writer

Jack Nicholson (b. 1937), actor; born in Neptune

Dorothy Parker (1893–1967), writer of ironic verse and short stories

Zebulon Montgomery Pike (1779–1813), army officer and explorer; discovered Pike's Peak

Robert Pinsky (b. 1940), U.S. poet laureate for an unprecedented three terms

Molly Pitcher (1744–1832), heroine of the Battle of Monmouth

Paul Robeson (1898–1976), singer and actor on stage and screen

Philip Roth (b. 1933), novelist

Frank Sinatra (1915–1998), singer and actor

Bruce Springsteen (b. 1949), rock star

John Travolta (b. 1954), actor

William Carlos Williams (1883–1963), pediatrician and Pulitzer Prize–winning poet

Edmund Wilson (1895–1972), editor, author, and critic

...and Great Places

Some interesting derivations of New Jersey place names.

Absecon A town and an inlet bear this name, probably from the Algonquian for "small water" (in contrast to the ocean).

Batsto From the Dutch word meaning "bath house."

Bayonne Named after the city in France, possibly with a pun in mind, since the city is, after all, on Upper New York Bay.

Bergen Named by Dutch settlers after Bergen-on-zoom, a city in their native Netherlands.

Cape May Named for a Dutch sea captain, Cornelius Jacobsen Mey, who sailed there in the early 17th century.

Elizabeth Named for Elizabeth Carteret, one of the original 17th-century settlers.

Hackensack From the name of an Indian village and tribe.

Irvington Named for the writer Washington Irving.

Kittatinny Mountains From an Algonquian word meaning "big-mountain-at."

Newark From a town name in England.

Orange The four Oranges (East, West, South, and plain Orange) may be derived from William, Prince of Orange (a Dutch title), but more likely come from an Indian name, Auronge.

Passaic Delaware Algonquian for "valley."

Perth Amboy From the Scottish city and county, Perth, combined with an Algonquian word meaning "something hollowed out," such as a valley.

Piscataway From an Algonquian term meaning "fork-(of)-river-at."

Princeton Named in 1724 as a compliment to the British royal family, and as a counterpart to a nearby Kingston.

Pulaski Honors the Polish Count Casimir Pulaski, one of George Washington's generals and a Revolutionary War hero.

Rahway A variant of "Rockaway," which originally meant "sandy place" in Algonquian.

Raritan A town and a river, both from an Algonquian name that means "stream overflows."

Secaucus From the Algonquian word meaning "river-little-at."

Teaneck Derived from the name of a local Dutch family, Teneyck.

Trenton Named for the founder, William Trent, in the early 18th century—one of the earliest examples of a developer naming a place after himself.

Hoboken From the name of a Belgian village, home of some early settlers.

NEW JERSEY BY THE SEASONS
A Perennial Calendar of Events and Festivals

Here is a selective listing of events that take place each year in the months noted;
we suggest calling ahead to local chambers of commerce for dates and details.

January

Camden
Three-dimensional Art Show
Exhibition at Steadman Gallery,
Rutgers Center for the Arts.

Trenton
Annual Science Event
New Jersey State Museum
offers experiments, workshops.

February

Atlantic City
Classic Car Show and Auction
600 classic cars and 1,000 booths
of auto-related items.

Sail Expo
State's biggest sailboat show.

Chester
Cabin Fever Celebration
Ice sculptures, chocolate houses
chase winter blues.

Somerset
New Jersey Flower & Garden Show
Annual showcase of landscaped
gardens, floral designs; lectures
and workshops.

March

Atlantic City
Atlantique City Spring Festival
World's largest indoor antiques
and collectibles show; also in
October.

Pennsauken
Train and Collectible Toy Show
The marketplace for toy trains;
at South Jersey Expo Center.

Seaside Heights
Leprechaun Contest
A chance to ride the Lepre-
chaun float in the St. Patrick's
Day parade.

Union City
The Passion Play
Oldest continuously running
production in the country.

April

Cape May
Spring Festival and Garden Weekend
Thousands of tulips, tours of
historic houses and gardens.

Lambertville
Shad Festival
Celebrates shad swimming up
the Delaware River, with juried
arts and crafts show, live music.

Montclair
One-Act Festival of New Jersey
Playwrights
Brings together well-known
and aspiring playwrights.

Newark
Essex County Cherry Blossom
Festival
Largest display in the U.S.

Seaside Heights
Easter Sunday Promenade
A chance to see and be seen on
the amusement park boardwalk.

May

Cape May Point
World Series of Birding
Birders vie to tally the most
different species.

Flemington
Lindbergh & Hauptmann:
The Trial of the Century
Live reenactment of the kid-
napping trial in historic
Hunterdon Courthouse.

Somerville
Tour of Somerville
Oldest continuous bike race in
the U.S.

Westampton
American Indian Arts Festival
Native American artists and
performers gather at Rankokus
Indian Reservation.

Wildwood
International Kite Festival
World's largest, three events.

June

Cape May
Music Festival
Month-long array of concerts
includes classical, pop, and jazz.

Jersey Shore Communities
Seafood Festivals
Throughout the summer, in Atlantic City, Belmar, other towns. Sample ocean delicacies.

Manalapan
Battle of Monmouth Reenactment
Longest infantry battle of the American Revolution, at Battlefield State Park.

Port Norris
Delaware Bay Day
Includes blue-crab races, seafood, oyster-shucking contest.

Trenton
Heritage Days
State's largest outdoor ethnic festival; music on four stages.

July

Cherry Hill
New Jersey State Fair

Hoboken
St. Ann's Italian Street Festival

Ocean City
Night in Venice
Boats and shoreline homes decked out for annual water parade.

Wildwood
Doo Wop Music Festival
Music and memorabilia, with 1950s headliners, crafts.

August

Atlantic City
Wedding of the Sea
Nationally renowned ocean blessing and mass.

East Rutherford
Hambletonian Day
America's premier championship harness race, in a country fair setting.

Ocean City
Baby Parade on the Boardwalk

Sussex
Sussex Air Show
World-class performers put vintage planes through death-defying maneuvers.

September

Atlantic City
Miss America Pageant; Boardwalk Parade

Jersey City
New Jersey Harbor Heritage Day
Maritime celebration with boats, clambake, sailing races.

New Brunswick
New Jersey Book Fair
Author appearances, music, bookmaking demonstrations.

Stanhope
Waterloo Village Antiques Fair
State's largest outdoor antiques show.

October

Bordentown and Chatsworth
Cranberry Festival
Celebrating the harvest with bog tours, entertainment.

Cape May
Victorian Week
A week of house tours, fashion shows, antiques, art and crafts.

Milford
Bed Race and Fall Festival
Features people-powered beds on Bridge Street; prizes for speed and originality.

November

Cherry Hill
South Jersey Fall Food & Wine Festival
Wines from local vintners; cuisine from area restaurants and food producers.

Waretown
New Jersey Devil Show
The devil himself shows up for country and bluegrass music.

West Orange
Christmas at Glenmont
See how Edison's family celebrated the holidays.

December

Cape May
Christmas in Cape May
Weekly performances of Dickens's *A Christmas Carol*, costumed carolers, and Christmas Candlelight House Tour.

Surf City
Miniature Art Exhibit
International juried show.

Titusville
George Washington Crossing the Delaware
His heroic journey of Christmas Day 1776 is reenacted at Washington Crossing State Park.

WHERE TO GO
Museums, Attractions, Gardens, and Other Arts Resources

Call for seasons and hours when open.

Museums

ART MUSEUM OF PRINCETON UNIVERSITY
McCormick Hall, Princeton, 609-258-3788
European, Chinese, pre-Columbian art; paintings, prints, photography.

ATLANTIC CITY ART CENTER & HISTORICAL MUSEUM
Garden Pier on the Boardwalk, Atlantic City, 609-347-5839
Three art galleries, and extensive displays tracing an island village's growth into a world-renowned resort.

BARNEGAT BAY DECOY AND BAYMEN'S MUSEUM
137 W. Main St. (Rt. 9), P.O. Box 520-8087, Tuckerton, 609-296-8868
Collections of shipbuilding and lifesaving equipment, carved decoys preserve the baymen's way of life.

GROUNDS FOR SCULPTURE
18 Fairgrounds Rd., Hamilton, 609-586-0616
This 22-acre park and museum has rotating exhibits of contemporary sculpture in a landscaped setting.

MONTCLAIR ART MUSEUM
3 S. Mountain Ave., Montclair, 973-746-5555
Continuing the legacy of 1890s artists' colony, with exhibits, tours, concerts, and classes.

MUSEUM OF AMERICAN GLASS
Wheaton Village, 1501 Glasstown Rd., Millville, 800-998-4552/609-825-6800
Over 7,500 beautiful glass objects; glass-blowing demonstrations at the 1888 Wheaton Glass Factory.

MUSEUM OF EARLY TRADES AND CRAFTS
Main St. & Green Village Rd., Madison, 973-377-2982
A hands-on view of the past.

NEW JERSEY HISTORICAL SOCIETY
52 Park Pl., Newark, 973-596-8500
Changing exhibits and family events bring the Garden State's history to life.

NEW JERSEY STATE MUSEUM AND PLANETARIUM
205 W. State St., Trenton, 609-292-6464/6308
Nation's oldest state museum (founded 1895) features 19th- and 20th-century American art, fossils, native American exhibits.

THE NEWARK MUSEUM
49 Washington St., Newark, 800-768-7886, 973-596-6550
Extensive collection of 18th- to 20th-century American paintings and sculpture; finest Tibetan art collection in the U.S.

RIPLEY'S BELIEVE IT OR NOT! MUSEUM
New York Ave. & Boardwalk, Atlantic City, 609-347-2001

TRASH MUSEUM, HACKENSACK MEADOWLANDS ENVIRONMENTAL CENTER
2 DeKorte Park Plaza, Lyndhurst, 201-460-8300
Designed for kids, an interactive depiction of where your garbage goes.

U.S.G.A. GOLF HOUSE MUSEUM
Liberty Corner Rd., Far Hills, 908-234-2300

Attractions

ATLANTIC CITY BOARDWALK
Atlantic City, 609-347-5300
First built in 1870, its six miles still offer saltwater taffy, amusement rides, and souvenirs, as well as the recent casinos.

Other boardwalks include those at Ocean Grove, with Victorian charm and spotless beaches (732-775-0035); Point Pleasant Beach with Jenkinson's Aquarium (732-892-1118); Ocean City, (800-232-2465); Wildwood, with more rides than any other boardwalk in the country (609-729-4000); and Cape May (609-884-5508).

CAPE MAY BIRD OBSERVATORY: CENTER FOR RESEARCH AND EDUCATION
600 Rt. 47 N., Cape May, 609-884-2736
Birding center; special activities during spring and fall migrations.

CATHEDRAL BASILICA OF THE SACRED HEART
89 Ridge St., Newark, 973-484-4600
Spectacular French Gothic cathedral with massive gargoyles, stained-glass windows, 9,500-pipe organ.

COWTOWN RODEO
780 Rt. 40, Woodstown, 609-769-3200
Features top rodeo talent from around the U.S., Saturday nights in summer.

EDISON NATIONAL HISTORIC SITE
Main St. & Lakeside Ave., West Orange, 973-736-0550
His estate and invention laboratory, with the first light bulb, phonograph, and motion picture equipment.

GINGERBREAD CASTLE
Off Rt. 23 N., P.O. Box 69, Hamburg, 973-827-1617

HISTORIC BATSTO VILLAGE
Wharton State Forest, Rt. 542, Batsto, 609-561-3262
Restored Pine Barrens village, produced most ammunition for American Revolution.

HISTORIC COLD SPRING VILLAGE
720 Rt. 9, Cape May, 609-898-2300
Blacksmith, tinsmith, potter, and weaver ply their trades in this typical 19th-century village.

LIBERTY STATE PARK
Exit 14B, NJ Turnpike, Morris Pesin Drive, 201-435-9499
Visitor center, nature trail, ferries to Ellis Island and Statue of Liberty.

LUCY THE ELEPHANT
Atlantic & Decatur Aves., Margate, 609-823-6473
She's the world's only elephant you can walk through.

MORRISTOWN NATIONAL HISTORICAL PARK
Information: Historic Morristown Visitors Center, 14 Elm St., Morristown, 201-993-1194
Preserves four sites of Washington's winter encampments: his headquarters at the Ford Mansion, Fort Nonsense, Jockey Hollow, and New Jersey Brigade.

NEW JERSEY SHAKESPEARE FESTIVAL
36 Madison Ave., Madison, 973-408-5600

NEW JERSEY STATE AQUARIUM
1 Riverside Dr., Camden, 888 GO FISH GO (888-463-4744)/609-365-3300
Over 4,000 water creatures of 500 species. "Ocean Base Atlantic" transports visitors to a Caribbean underwater habitat.

NORTHLANDZ
495 Hwy. 202, Flemington, 908-782-4022
Miniature Great American Railway: 125 trains travel on 8 miles of tracks through towns and cities, mountains and valleys. World-class doll collection.

STONE HARBOR BIRD SANCTUARY
3rd Ave. & 114th St., Stone Harbor, 609-368-5102
WETLANDS INSTITUTE
1075 Stone Harbor Blvd., Stone Harbor, 609-368-1211
Both sites are paradise for birders, with nature trails through the wetlands and an observation tower.

WATERLOO VILLAGE

525 Waterloo Rd. in Allamuchy State Park, Stanhope, 973-347-0900

Living history site hosts festivals throughout the year.

Homes and Gardens

LEONARD J. BUCK GARDEN

11 Layton Rd., Far Hills, 908-234-2677

Rock gardener's paradise: 33 acres of alpine plants in a natural gorge, with bog, meadow, and woodland.

COLONIAL PARK GARDENS

Mettler's Rd., East Millstone, 908-234-2677

Highlight is All-American Selections Rose Garden with 4,000 roses. (View them in June, before Japanese beetles arrive in July.)

DRUMTHWACKET

354 Stockton St., Princeton, 609-683-0057

Official governor's residence, this 1834 Greek Revival mansion was built for Charles S. Olden, governor during the Civil War.

DUKE GARDENS

Rt. 206, 17 mi. north of Princeton, 1-1/2 mi. south of Somerville, 908-722-3700

Eleven greenhouses re-create gardens of different cultures and periods. Guided tours only; advance reservations required.

EMLEN PHYSICK ESTATE MUSEUM

1048 Washington St., Cape May, 609-884-5404

Glimpse daily life of a Victorian household at elaborate 18-room mansion built in 1879.

HERMITAGE/JOHN ROSENCRANTZ HOUSE

335 N. Franklin Tpk., Ho-Ho-Kus, 201-445-8311

Victorian events, including lavish Christmas festivities, are held year-round at this elegant 1847 Gothic Revival house.

HISTORIC MORVEN

55 Stockton St., Princeton, 609-683-4495

Former home of Richard Stockton, signer of the Declaration of Independence, and official governor's residence from 1953 to 1981.

LEAMING'S RUN GARDENS & COLONIAL FARM

1845 Rt. 9 N, Swainton, 609-465-5871

Largest annual garden in U.S., with 25 different gardens on 30 acres, colonial whaler's farm.

REEVES-REED ARBORETUM

165 Hobart Ave., Summit, 908-273-8787

A 12-acre jewel with spring daffodils, blazing autumn woodlands.

SKYLANDS BOTANICAL GARDEN

Ringwood State Park, Morris Rd., Ringwood, 973-962-7527/7031

State's official botanical garden; 125 acres contain worldwide plant collection of Clarence McKenzie Lewis.

STEUBEN HOUSE

New Bridge Landing Historic Park, River Edge, 201-487-1739

Built in 1713, important in the Revolutionary War.

WALT WHITMAN HOUSE

330 Mickle Blvd., Camden, 609-964-5383

Former home of the great poet displays manuscripts, photographs, and memorabilia.

Other Resources

NEW JERSEY DIVISION OF TRAVEL & TOURISM

20 W. State St., P.O. Box 826, Trenton 08625, 800-537-7397 (to request literature), 609-292-2470

CREDITS

The authors have made every effort to reach copyright holders of text and owners of illustrations, and wish to thank those individuals and institutions that permitted the reprinting of text or the reproduction of works in their collections. Credits not listed in the captions are provided below. References are to page numbers; the designations a, b, and c indicate position of illustrations on pages.

Text

Bruce Springsteen Music: "Born to Run" by Bruce Springsteen. Copyright © 1975 by Bruce Springsteen (ASCAP).

Farrar, Straus & Giroux: Excerpt from "The Woods from Hog Wallow" from *The Pine Barrens* by John McPhee. Copyright © 1968 and copyright renewed © 1993 by John McPhee. Excerpt from "Gloucestershire" from *The Counterlife* by Philip Roth. Copyright © 1986 by Philip Roth. Both, reprinted by permission.

Henry Holt & Company: *Twin Rivers: The Raritan and the Passaic* by Harry Emerson Wildes. Copyright © 1943 by Harry Emerson Wildes.

Alfred A. Knopf: *The Poorhouse Fair* by John Updike. Copyright © 1958 by John Updike. *Time Present, Time Past* by Bill Bradley. Copyright © Bill Bradley. Both, used with permission.

Paul Simon Music: "America," words and music by Paul Simon. Copyright © 1968 by Paul Simon.

New Directions Publishing Corp.: *Paterson* by William Carlos Williams. Copyright © 1948 by William Carlos Williams. Reprinted by permission.

Prometheus Books: *Christie Whitman for the People: A Political Biography* by Sandy McClure (Amherst, NY: Prometheus Books). Copyright © 1996 by Prometheus Books. Reprinted by permission.

Rutgers University Press: *A New Jersey Reader* by Henry Charlton Beck. Copyright © 1961 by Rutgers, The State University. Reprinted by permission.

Simon & Schuster: *This Side of Paradise* by F. Scott Fitzgerald (New York: Charles Scribner's Sons, 1920). Copyright © 1920 by Charles Scribner's Sons. Renewed © 1948 by

Zelda Fitzgerald. Reprinted with permission of Scribner, a division of Simon & Schuster, Inc.

Warner-Chappell, Inc.: "Before the Music Ends," words and music by Gordon Jenkins. Copyright © 1980.

Illustrations

DAVID AHLSTED: **22** *Maurice River and Farmlands*, 1995. Oil on canvas. 60 x 72"; AMERICAN SWEDISH HISTORICAL SOCIETY: **28b** Johan Printz. Oil on canvas. 41¼ x 31¾"; JOHN BAEDER: **44** *Tick Tock Diner*, 1983. Oil on canvas. 27 x 40"; BRUCE BENNETT: **17b**; JACQUELINE CHESLEY: **34** *Flower Farm #1*, 1994. Oil on paper. 50 x 38"; WALTER CHOROSZEWSKI: **11**; **15b**; **19**; **23a**; **33**; **45**; **51b**; **56a**; **58a**; **59a**; **60a**; **61**; **89** Hoboken; ANN COOPER AND CAMEO APPEARANCES, NY: **62** *Down the Shore*, 1999. Watercolor on paper. 15 x 11"; TIM DALY: **83b** *West of Routes 1 & 9*, 1986. Acrylic on canvas. 44 x 72"; THE ESTATE OF JOHN MARIN/RICHARD YORK GALLERY, NEW YORK: **5** *Autumn, New Jersey* by John Marin, 1913. Watercolor on paper. 13¾ x 16¾"; LISBETH FIRMIN AND CAMEO APPEARANCES, NEW YORK: **49b** *Holland Tunnel*, 1999. Gouache. 5 x 5", GROUNDS FOR SCULPTURE: **53b** *Déjeuner Déjà Vu* by J. Seward Johnson, Jr., 1994. Cast bronze. 62 x 132 x 360" Photo Ricardo Barros, HACKETT-FREEDMAN GALLERY, SAN FRANCISCO: **84** *The Black Chair* by Robert Birmelin, 1994. Acrylic on canvas. 48 x 36"; ROBERT HEIDE AND JOHN GILMAN: **10**; **13a**; **13b**; **14a**; **15c**; **17a**; **36a**; **36b**; **37**; **38**; **63a**; **63b**; **65b**; **67a**; **74b**; **78b** *Allen Ginsberg Thumbprint Portrait* by Hoop, c. 1996; **85b** *Four + Fore = ?* by Hoop, 1998. Dismantled; **86a** Lucy; KELLY/MOONEY: **20**; **31b**; **58b**; **86c** Atlantic City, **87b** Gingerbread Castle; **87c** Waterloo Village; BARBARA KULICKE: **85a** *A Square of the Gap*, 1997. Oil on slate. 18 x 18"; VALERI LARKO: **83a** *Spiral, Jersey City*, 1998. Oil on canvas. 46 x 30"; LENOX, INC.: **39a**; LIBRARY OF CONGRESS: **27b** Tishcohan; **46** Thomas Edison and son, **47** *Annabelle Butterfly Dance*; LIONEL, L.L.C.: **41a**; MARLBOROUGH GALLERY, INC., NEW YORK: **48** *S-Bend in an Elevated Section of the New Jersey Turnpike* by Rackstraw Downes, 1996. Oil on canvas. 18 x 94½"; THE METROPOLITAN MUSEUM OF ART, NEW YORK: **18** *The Palisades* by John Hill after William Guy Wall, 1823–24. Hand- and plate-colored aquatint. 18 x 24¼". The Edward W. C. Arnold Collection of New York Prints, Maps and Pictures. Bequest of Edward W. C. Arnold, 1954

(54.90.601); **30** *Washington Crossing the Delaware* by Emanuel
Gottlieb Leutze, 1851. Oil on canvas. 149 x 255". Gift of
John Stewart Kennedy, 1897 (97.34); MONTCLAIR ART
MUSEUM: **21** *The Delaware Water Gap* by George Inness, 1857.
Oil on canvas. 32 x 52¼". Permanent collection. Gift of
Mrs. F. G. Herman Fayen in memory of Mr. Fayen, 1930.2;
81a *Fox Leaf* by Vivian McDuffie, 1995. Oil on paper. 21½ x
30". Gift of Robert and Joanne Mitchell in honor of Jessie
Campbell, 1999.3.1. Photo Peter Jacobs; **81b** *Early Autumn* by
George Inness, 1888. Oil on canvas. 30 x 45". Museum
purchase; funds provided by Dr. Arthur Hunter in mem-
ory of Ethel Parsons Hunter, the Valley Foundation, and
Acquisition Fund, 1960.28; **80** *Snake Hill on the Jersey Meadows*
by Charles Parsons, 1871. Oil on canvas. 13 x 32". Gift of
Ethel Parsons Hunter, 1958.26; MUSEUM OF FINE ARTS,
BOSTON: **24** *Long Branch, New Jersey* by Winslow Homer,
1869. Oil on canvas. 16 x 21¾". The Hayden Collection;
NATIONAL GEOGRAPHIC SOCIETY IMAGE COLLECTION: **12a**
New Jersey flag. Illustration by Marilyn Dye Smith; **12b**
Eastern goldfinch and common meadow violet. Illustra-
tion by Robert E. Hynes; NATIONAL MUSEUM OF AMERI-
CAN ART/ART RESOURCE: **40** *Newark* by Stuart Davis, 1910.
Oil on wood. 9 x 13"; NEAL PETERS COLLECTION: **73a; 88**
Meryl Streep; NEW JERSEY HISTORICAL SOCIETY: **26** *Henry
Hudson landing on the New Jersey shore of the Hudson River* by R. W.
Weir, c. 1857; **29** *Philip Carteret appointed Governor of the colony of
New Jersey, landing at Newark Bay in 1665* by Howard Pyle, c.
1904–07; **77a** News headlines; NEW JERSEY NEWSPHOTOS:
39b; 41b; 65a; 70a; 70b; 86b RCA's "Little Nipper"; **87a**
Cowtown Rodeo; NEW JERSEY STATE COUNCIL ON THE
ARTS: **1** *Cityscape* by Hughie Lee-Smith, 1988. Oil on can-
vas. 60 x 120". Photo Dan Dragan; **53a** *Five Flying Fish* by
Jonathan Borofsky, 1997. Hand painted fiberglass, alu-
minum, and fabric. 12 x 18'; NEWARK PUBLIC LIBRARY: **42a;
43;** THE NOYES MUSEUM OF ART: *Miss America Float* by
Malcah Zeldis, 1989. Oil on board. 25 x 31". 1997.10; PAPER
MILL PLAYHOUSE: **74a;** PRIVATE COLLECTION: **2** *Dancing on the
George Washington Bridge* by Faith Ringgold, 1988. Acrylic on
canvas with printed and dyed pieces. 68 x 68"; **12c; 16;**
SALANDER-O'REILLY GALLERIES, NEW YORK: **82** *Factories in
New Jersey* by Paul Weingarten, 1993. Oil on canvas. 52 x
66"; SALEM COUNTY HISTORICAL SOCIETY: **28a** *Ivey Point*
by William Patterson, c. mid-19th century. Oil on canvas.

16 x 20"; WILLIAM WEGMAN: **52** Selections from *Six Scenic
Scenes*, 1997. Iris prints. 64 x 49" each. Atlantic City Con-
vention Center Installation. Installation made possible by
the Public Building Arts Inclusion Act of 1978. The Arts
Inclusion program is administered by the New Jersey
State Council on the Arts. Funding was provided by the
New Jersey Sports and Exposition Authority; WHITNEY
MUSEUM OF AMERICAN ART, NEW YORK: **9** *Space Motive, a
N.J. Valley* by Oscar Bluemner, c. 1917–18. Oil on canvas.
30½ x 40½"; ALICE STEER WILSON: **66** *High Summer*, 1993.
Watercolor on paper. 12 x 20"

Acknowledgements

Walking Stick Press wishes to thank our project staff:
Nancy Friedman, Miriam Lewis, Joanna Lynch, Thérèse
Martin, Laurie Donaldson, Inga Lewin, Tena Scalph, Kristi
Hein, and Mark Woodworth.

For other assistance with *New Jersey*, we are especially
grateful to: Lindsay Kefauver, Natalie Goldstein, Valerie
Vogel, Monica Murphy, Alys Petsoff of the Monclair Art
Museum, Irina Peris of the New Jersey Historical Society,
Tom Moran of the State Council on the Arts, and Walter
Choroszewski.